Graduate Citizens?

What does being a citizen mean to today's students?

Following the introduction of student loans and tuition fees, the situation of students and new graduates has changed considerably. Set in this context, *Graduate Citizens?* is a thought-provoking and insightful look at the current generation of students' attitudes towards citizenship and matters of social and moral responsibility.

Drawing on small-scale case studies of students in two universities, the authors explore students' changing sense of citizenship against the backdrop of recent changes in higher education. It addresses students' approaches to being in debt, the role of their families in providing support and their attitudes towards careers. Questioning the claim that the current generation of students is politically apathetic, this book shows that they are in fact socially concerned, though distanced from official, mainstream politics. It investigates students' responses to such political and economic phenomena as globalisation and the ever-increasing promotion of market forces.

Graduate Citizens? illuminates and explores the links between reforms in higher education, student experience of university and issues of citizenship. It poses questions about the condition and future of citizenship in Britain and discusses the implications for citizenship education.

John Ahier is a Research Fellow in the Faculty of Education and Language Studies at the Open University. **John Beck** and **Rob Moore** are members of the Faculty of Education, University of Cambridge; John is Education Team Chair and Rob is Reader in Sociology of Education at Homerton College.

Graduate Citizens?

Issues of citizenship and higher education

John Ahier, John Beck and Rob Moore

rf RoutledgeFalmer
Taylor & Francis Group

LONDON AND NEW YORK

First published 2003
by RoutledgeFalmer
11 New Fetter Lane, London EC4P 4EE

Simultaneously published in the USA and Canada
by RoutledgeFalmer
29 West 35th Street, New York, NY 10001

RoutledgeFalmer is an imprint of the Taylor & Francis Group

© 2003 John Ahier, John Beck and Rob Moore

British Library Cataloguing in Publication Data
A catalogue record for this book is available from the British
Library

Library of Congress Cataloging in Publication Data
A catalog record for this book has been requested

ISBN 0-415-25722-0 (HB)
ISBN 0-415-25723-9 (PB)

Contents

Acknowledgements

The qualitative data used in Part II of this book was generated from the Choosing and Using Higher Education project. The authors would like to acknowledge the generous help given to this project by both Homerton College, Cambridge and the Faculty of Education and Language Studies at the Open University.

We wish to thank Emma Creighton for her work as interviewer on the project over two years.

We are also grateful to colleagues at Anglia Polytechnic University for their interest and support.

List of abbreviations

APU	Anglia Polytechnic University
AUT	The Association of University Teachers
CCCS	Centre for Contemporary Cultural Studies (University of Birmingham)
CIHE	Council for Industry and Higher Education
CVCP	Committee of Vice Chancellors and Principals
DEA	Department of Economic Affairs
DFE	Department for Education
DFEE	Department for Education and Employment
EMU	European Monetary Union
EU	European Union
IES	Institute of Employment Studies
IPPR	Institute for Public Policy Research
MO	Mass Observation
NCIHE	National Committee of Inquiry into Higher Education
NGOs	Non-Governmental Organisations
NHS	National Health Service
NUS	National Union of Students
OECD	Organisation for European Co-operation and Development
OFSTED	Office for Standards in Education
PCFC	Polytechnics and Colleges Funding Council
QCA	Qualifications and Curriculum Authority
UK	United Kingdom

Introduction
Citizenship and higher education in modern Britain

Now seems a good time for those with an interest in citizenship to look at current developments within higher education. While in the past the role of universities in relation to 'nation building' was widely acknowledged, because of the small numbers of students involved, this was more concerned with the production of indigenous elites than with the education of an active, diverse citizenry. However, as universities lost the financial basis of their autonomy, with larger amounts of public money supporting a wider variety of higher education institutions, governments in many countries tried to identify the broader social functions of higher education. In Britain, the Robbins Report was a turning point in this regard when it declared that 'the transmission of a common culture and standards of citizenship' was one of the fundamental aims of higher education (Committee on Higher Education 1963: 7). The report also proposed that what had been a loose set of institutions with different histories should be conceptualised henceforth as a national *system* of higher education:

> Higher education is so obviously and rightly of great public concern, and so large a proportion of its finance is provided in one way or another from the public purse, that it is difficult to defend the continued absence of co-ordinating principles and of a general conception of objectives; . . . the needs of the present and still more of the future demand that there be a system.
>
> (ibid.: 5)

If the Robbins Report represented a high point in modern national higher education, more recently, the situation has

become less clear. Although the concept of 'mass higher education' could be seen as an over-statement, recruitment has broad-
ened and deepened beyond anything envisaged by Robbins. Yet
identifying what might be regarded as the more noble social aims
of a higher education system is now more difficult. Part of the
reason for this may be that as recruitment has expanded, governments have wanted to make the new participants fund more of
their own higher education. Emphasis now tends to be put on
mutual, instrumental benefits, with higher education represented
as a good investment for both the individual and the economy. At
the same time, the universities themselves are increasingly being
detached from the nation by market forces which require that
they sell their services globally.

   To explore some of the problems and possibilities of this
changed situation, in Part I of this book we first examine various
aspects of contemporary debates about citizenship in general;
second, we consider certain respects in which citizenship in
Britain may have a distinctive character, and third, we explore
some of the ways in which contemporary developments in higher
education could be seen as part of the reconstruction of the
citizen. After comparing a variety of approaches to theorising citizenship, we consider in relation to the British case three 'models'
which seem to have been most significant and which are still influential. Of these different models, our preference for what we term
'social national citizenship' leads us to consider the possibility
that this form of citizenship is currently faced with a number of
challenges and threats. These have their origins in various aspects
of contemporary social, economic and political change. Having
examined such challenges at the general level, we focus more
particularly on the effects of certain developments in the financing, control and ethos of *universities*. The central question posed is
whether, despite political anxieties about such things as the low
turn-out at elections and loss of civic engagement, crucial national
institutions like the universities are now being directed to
promote predominantly individualistic and instrumental ways of
life and conceptions of citizenship. To some of those working
within these institutions, recent policies have often seemed antag-
onistic to the earlier social aims of higher education. However, we
identify and discuss a range of reservations about the effects
attributed to such policies by such commentators and then,
in Part II, we go on to explore whether contemporary under-

graduates are really forsaking social national citizenship in favour of heightened economic individualism and more strongly privatised orientations.

Drawing upon a small-scale empirical piece of research among students in English universities, we present in Part II, students' perspectives on their future lives as employees and citizens. Two major sets of issues are highlighted. First, although these students certainly grew up during the years of the Thatcher and then the Major governments in the UK, it was very clear from our conversations with them that they were not, in any unqualified sense, 'Thatcher's children'. Although they were among the first generation of UK university students to experience the effects of the introduction of both student loans and tuition fees, they had clearly *not* embraced the proffered identities of 'investors in themselves' or 'entrepreneurs of their own futures'. It was, however, also clear that many of them did feel a sense of distance and disengagement from 'official politics' and in that respect they may appear to typify popular stereotypes of being members of an 'apathetic generation'. Second, however, their comments also revealed a strong sense of what we have called socially grounded 'mutuality' – a set of concerns about social justice and fairness, informing their sense of relatedness to others. In these respects they are clearly people who are both socially conscious and concerned, even though they almost never employed a vocabulary of political citizenship to express such sentiments. These tentative findings lead us to conclude that there are grounds for some optimism about the graduate citizens of the future, at least when compared to the forebodings of those commentators who deplore the supposed detachment and rootlessness of the current generation of students.

Part I

Citizenship and higher education in modern Britain

Some reflections

Chapter I

Citizenship in Britain
Models and identities

1.1 Citizenship in Britain: the sound of silence?

With effect from September 2002, 'Citizenship' became a Foundation Subject of the National Curriculum in England (slightly varied arrangements obtain in Wales and significantly different curricular provision exists in Scotland and Northern Ireland). This development is in one sense a noteworthy victory for those who, over many years, have campaigned to persuade generally reluctant governments to find space in the curriculum for what has variously been termed 'civics', 'political literacy', and most recently, 'citizenship education'.

Yet, as numerous commentators have observed, the language of citizenship and its cognates appear to have little resonance for many people in Britain. In a recent article comparing approaches to citizenship education in Britain and the USA, Elizabeth Frazer remarks:

> It is interesting and notable that 'citizenship' is the term that has invariably been used by promoters of political education ... This is curious because it is equally notable that it either lacks salience for significant sections of the intended audience, or evokes an antipathetic response. In comparative research in England and the USA, Crewe and his colleagues found that English respondents did not use the concept 'citizenship' themselves in connection with their own political identities; for some there was clear discomfort with its connotations of 'foreignness'.
>
> (Frazer 2000: 92)

Frazer amplifies her point by citing Wilkins' (1999) survey of Postgraduate Certificate in Education students in two large English teacher training institutions:

> like Crewe's respondents, this group have difficulties with the language of citizenship. The idea of a 'good citizen' prompted negative images such as 'disgusted of Tunbridge Wells', 'stiff upper lip and bowler hat', 'neighbourhood watch and writing letters to the parish council' – that is, stereotypes of a particular kind of middle class-ness ... When at the end of their course these respondents were asked about 'teaching citizenship' they seemed even more uncertain and sceptical than they had been at the beginning of the study, (not least) because of continuing vagueness about what citizenship is.
>
> (ibid.: 96)

An even more recent survey, this time of practising teachers, suggests that insofar as English teachers employ a discourse of citizenship at all, it is highly depoliticised and tends to focus on participation in voluntary activities within the local community:

> Among primary school teachers there is little evidence of citizenship as directed to the political sphere. There is some evidence among secondary school teachers of citizenship as bearing upon matters of a more ostensibly political nature. But common to all our teachers is the sense that good citizenship is primarily about meeting the obligations we stand under towards fellow members of a community.
>
> (Davies et al. 1999: 44)

The work of Arnot and her colleagues, based on another sample of trainee teachers also surveyed in 1995, corroborates this finding:

> There is no strong evidence from this small sample that the new generation of teachers in the UK are able to articulate discourses of citizenship which are personally meaningful or liberatory. On the whole, the English and Welsh student teachers held impoverished notions of political discourse, and made critical or even cynical references to the moral superficiality or corruption of politicians.
>
> (Arnot 1997: 288, see also Arnot et al. 1995)

Of course, it is possible to argue that the lack of a strong tradition of citizenship *education* in Britain (and more particularly in England) is itself part of the explanation of this lack of ease with the language of citizenship – and there must be some truth in this. But it is surely more likely that *both* absences reflect some more fundamental peculiarity of the English,[1] or at any rate, of English culture and the history of its political institutions. A frequently canvassed explanation here is the contention that citizenship in the UK has been organised around a deep-rooted positioning of Britons as passive *subjects* rather than as citizens. Bryan Turner's influential comparative typology of citizenship, for example, locates British citizenship, in contrast to citizenship in France or the USA, precisely as 'passive' – the defining characteristic being that citizenship in Britain developed 'from above' not from below:

> the constitutional settlement of 1688 created the British citizen as the British subject, that is a legal personality whose indelible social rights are constituted by a monarch sitting in parliament. The notion of citizen-as-subject indicates clearly the relatively extensive notion of social rights but also the passive character of British civil institutions. The defeat of absolutism in the settlement of 1688 left behind a core of institutions (the Crown, the Church, the House of Lords, and traditional attitudes about the family and private life) which continued to dominate British life until the destructive force of the First and Second World Wars brought British culture eventually and reluctantly into the modern world.
>
> (Turner 1990: 207–8)

For our purposes, two points are particularly worth highlighting from this quotation. The first is that for a significant proportion of Britons, subjective identities rooted in a feeling of occupying their proper place in a legitimate ordered hierarchy were indeed central to what citizenship meant. A proud albeit equivocal sense of being a subject within a monarchical state and an imperial nation *was* the way in which their attachment to their society was most strongly and coherently felt, even if it was not for the most part formulated in terms of a *vocabulary* of being a 'subject'. For a perhaps dwindling proportion of UK citizens, something of this kind is probably still the case (we shall examine this further in due course). The second point to highlight, however, is that, as Turner suggests, Britain's tardy transition to modernity significantly *changed* not only the underlying reality of British citizenship but also the terms in which most citizens conceived of their membership of their society and nation.

The *contemporary* situation in the UK seems exceptionally complex. As the research data we reported earlier suggests, citizenship is elusive: there appears to be a lack of a shared vocabulary in which conceptions relating to citizenship can be thought or expressed while the overt vocabulary of citizenship and its cognates may actually be an obstacle to uncovering what respondents really think about their social membership and its relation to politics. This situation poses perplexing problems for those interested in researching citizenship. For example, the commonly employed research approach that simply 'confronts' respondents with questions couched directly in the language of citizenship, may fail to uncover the complexity and ambiguity of respondents' understanding and feelings about this area of their lives. An instructive example is the 1999 study we have already cited by Davies *et al.* One major source of data for this research was a forced-choice questionnaire in which teachers were asked to express varying degrees of agreement or disagreement with statements grouped under such headings as: 'the following characteristics are important qualities of a good citizen', and 'the following have influenced *my* citizenship' (ibid.: 32–4). While, as we have seen, this approach produced some interesting and worthwhile results, there remains a range of questions about the information and understandings which a methodology of this kind is *not* likely to uncover, as well as the risk that such direct questioning may produce potentially distorted accounts of the ways in which respondents think about these aspects of their lives – accounts which, moreover, are likely to be distorted in unknown ways.

Implicit in these observations is a key point. If we are to make much progress in understanding the elusive character of citizenship in modern Britain, it is essential to distinguish two levels of analysis: (a) the underlying political and constitutional reality of citizenship; and (b) the subjective constructs in terms of which citizens think and express their sense of social membership and attachment to larger social groupings, including but not only their sense of membership of society as a whole – in other words the *identity* aspect of citizenship. Both these aspects, taken together, constitute the social reality of citizenship – but particularly in the British case, they have to be painstakingly disentangled.

1.2 The political and constitutional reality of citizenship

It seems to be true that even at the level of *theoretical* discourse, citizenship as an explicit category is, as Geoff Mulgan has put it, 'one of those words which goes in cycles . . .; in some periods it lies dormant, but then at others it becomes a prism through which we think about our relationships to each other and to the state' (Mulgan 1994, quoted in Faulks 1998: 1). Other recent commentators have similarly remarked on the fluctuating academic fortunes of the concept:

> In 1978 it could be confidently stated that 'the concept of citizenship has gone out of fashion among political thinkers' (Van Gunsteren 1978: 9). By 1990 Derek Heater claimed that citizenship had become the 'buzzword' amongst thinkers on all points of the political spectrum (Heater 1990: 293).
>
> (Kymlicka and Norman 2000: 5)

There is now a strong consensus that since around 1980, there has been a burgeoning of academic interest in citizenship across a variety of disciplines, both in the UK and internationally. In addition, in Britain, 'all major political parties and many pressure groups have evoked the concept, either to lend focus to their policies or as a goal to be struggled for' (Faulks 1998: 1).

Notwithstanding this waxing and waning of theoretical debate and political 'take-up' however, it is important to emphasise that, at least in modern democratic societies, citizenship has a social reality – arising from its political and constitutional institutionalisation – which is enduring and pivotal. It is, of course, not the *same* citizenship in all societies (nor in the same society at different times). But, *pace* Mulgan, citizenship is *not* merely 'a prism through which we *think* about our relations to each other and to the state' (our italics), it is, rather, an underlying source of structuration which *shapes* certain of our relationships to one another, to the state, to institutions external to the state, as well as to those who are non-citizens. As Turner has put it:

Citizenship may be defined as that set of practices (juridical, political, economic and cultural) which define a person as a competent member of society, and which as a consequence shape the flow of resources to persons and social groups.

(1993: 2)

This kind of strongly sociological definition is important – at least for our purposes. For while as an *analytical* concept, citizenship can be employed to describe, analyse and compare these practices and relationships as they exist in different societies and at different times, the practices themselves and the institutions, legislation, etc. which underpins them in any particular instance, are a social reality and have real and determinate effects – not least, that specific forms of citizenship shape particular kinds of citizens, even when they do not identify themselves as such! Such a sociological definition, as Turner points out, has a further merit: it 'should help us to understand the dynamic social construction of citizenship which changes historically as a consequence of political struggles' (ibid.: 2), i.e. *competing* models of citizenship can themselves be the stake in such political contests.[2]

The most fundamental general elements of citizenship appear to include the following:

- *universality*, in the sense that the rights, obligations, etc. of citizenship apply equally (except where legitimately restricted) to all who are included as citizens, at least in principle;
- such 'universality', however, implies a *criterion of exclusion – defining both the external and internal boundaries of the application of citizenship*; externally, this primarily has reference to the nation–state (though it is arguable that with the emergence of trans-national entities such as the European Community, forms of overlapping citizenship may be emerging);[3] internally it has to do with issues such as which sections of a population are enfranchised or not (e.g. the history of the chronic exclusion of women from political citizenship in many ostensibly democratic polities);
- a set of legally defined and defensible *rights or entitlements* many of which, as Hogan (1997) has emphasised, are also crucial *protections*, e.g. civil liberties, certain welfare entitlements in regimes of social citizenship, etc.;
- a set of legally sanctioned *obligations* which citizens (or certain

categories of citizens) may not evade without penalty; examples may include obligations to pay taxes, the requirement to be available for military service, the requirement to vote in certain elections, etc.;

- a set of normatively sanctioned *responsibilities or virtues* which form part of what is held to constitute 'good citizenship' within particular conceptions of citizenship; Rawls' principles of public reasonableness and reciprocity are one currently influential example (Rawls 1993 and 1999).

All forms of citizenship in modern democratic states exhibit these formal characteristics. But, as the discussion so far has suggested, it is the more specific and substantive ways in which citizenship is institutionalised which have the most significant and determinate consequences for citizens' lives, as well as for their sense of political identity and social membership

In trying to advance our understanding of citizenship in Britain, it will be helpful to distinguish three distinct 'models' of citizenship which have shaped the reality of citizenship – even when this reality has not generally been thought of in terms of forms of citizenship. At this stage of the discussion, we shall distinguish these models primarily in terms of their objective, institutionalised characteristics – though some reference to questions of identity will be unavoidable.

1.2.1 *Citizens-as-subjects*

As we have noted, the category of 'subject' has often been set *in opposition* to that of 'citizen' in discussions of British citizenship. Thus the historian David Cannadine has recently contrasted 'the United States, where the inhabitants are citizens' with 'the United Kingdom, where the inhabitants are still subjects' (1998: 53–4). However, as we have also seen, Bryan Turner treats 'citizen-as-subject' as a distinct *type* of citizenship. And it is significant that Cannadine himself, when he comes to elaborate upon what shaped the much less deferential mentality typical of US citizens, actually focuses upon a set of *institutional and constitutional* differences between the two societies, resulting from the radical changes put in place in the USA after 1776:

However limited may have been the hierarchy which originated in colonial America, the founding fathers deliberately rejected and overthrew it by abolishing primogeniture and by declaring titles illegal. And this anti-hierarchical impulse was strengthened by the subsequent failure of the federalists to create a 'natural' aristocracy or to entrench it in the Senate. The American Revolution ... *did* assault political dependency, ... *did* outlaw formal distinctions of status, and by so doing, it *did* create a new sort of society and a new way of looking at society, increasingly unlike that in England.

(Cannadine 1998: 53, italics in the original)

These characteristics are in marked contrast to those which Turner, as well as numerous other commentators, have highlighted as historically underpinning British citizenship: the monarchy, political sovereignty in the constitutional form of 'the Crown in parliament', an hereditary aristocracy with political power long entrenched within the upper house of a bi-cameral legislature, an established Church, the absence of a written constitution or a bill of rights, the elaboration of a hierarchically arranged apparatus of titles and honours bestowed on individuals 'from above', etc. And as we shall argue at greater length in due course, in the UK, it was precisely these *institutional* features which played a key part in shaping the distinctive 'citizen-as-subject' identity which proved to be so exceptionally long-lived, if never hegemonic, among the British people.

1.2.2 Marshallian social citizenship

Famously, T. H. Marshall's celebrated (1949) lecture *Citizenship and Social Class* set out a grand narrative in which the emergence of a *social* element of citizenship was represented as the (still uncompleted) outcome of twentieth-century struggles to *enlarge* the scope of citizenship rights and make formal rights of civic and political citizenship more effective (Marshall 1950). Marshall's social citizenship required, and for a time helped to legitimise, a major expansion of the role of the social democratic state in extending certain forms of social security, as well as a range of social entitlements such as 'free' health care and 'free' education – extending these precisely *as* rights of citizenship. Marshall proposed this conception of citizenship, embedded within the context of 'the hyphenated society' of democratic-welfare-capitalism (ibid.: 131), as a superior alternative to either Marxian social revolution or unfettered free-market competition. Moreover, most commentators now accept that notwithstanding the quasi-evolutionary character of his three-stage schema of successively emerging civic, political and social citizenship, Marshall did *not* regard the development of social citizenship as an immanent characteristic of late capitalism as Giddens (1982) once misleadingly implied. Rather, as Turner has argued, Marshall was acutely aware of 'the contingent importance of wartime conditions on the development of social policy' (1990: 192–3) and, as Hindess has shown, although Marshall saw post-war British society as based upon a compromise between the 'moral' principles of social citizenship and 'amoral' capitalist class relations, he was perfectly clear that this balance might prove impossible to maintain and that it might tilt in either direction (1987: 35–6).

Despite this awareness of the historically contingent character of social citizenship on the part of its most celebrated advocate, Marshallian citizenship was, nevertheless, associated with the relatively stable period of consensus politics in which, at least for a generation of British citizens, the social element of citizenship (even if not generally thought of in that language) became a key part of the taken-for-granted backdrop of everyday existence – a backdrop against which individual life-plans were formulated and family decision-making took place. As Nicholas Rose has put it, in a passage which brings out both the co-operative and the coercive elements of this 'settlement':

> [I]t . . . seemed possible to bind all strata and classes into an agreement for social progress of which the state was, to a greater or lesser extent . . . the guarantor. This image of social progress through gradual amelioration of hardship and improvement of conditions of life won out over the image of social revolution on the one hand and the image of unfettered competition on the other. The social state would have the role of shaping and co-ordinating the strategies which would oblige all partners, no longer antagonists, to work towards and facilitate social progress.
>
> (1999a: 135)

1.2.3 Neo-liberal citizenship

Neo-liberal citizenship emerged as part of a sustained and calculated endeavour to dismantle and discredit social citizenship and 'welfarism', which were depicted as the source of the twin evils of 'dependency culture' and endemic 'producer dominance' within state services, allegedly making these services arrogant, inefficient and unresponsive to the wishes of clients. The critique, many aspects of which were articulated from the Left as well as the Right (CCCS 1981), is familiar and need not be rehearsed here. The neo-liberal restructuring of the social democratic 'settlement' in the UK involved three main elements: first, the programme of outright privatisation (and in some cases the politically motivated destruction) of state-owned industries; second, a reconstruction of the relationships between public sector service providers, citizens as the clients of those services, and the state; and third, a work of identity construction seeking to shape a new kind of 'citizen' identity. We shall discuss only the second and third of these – which are, in any case, inter-related.

There is a broad consensus that these developments involved a 'marketization of citizenship' (Freedland 2001) or what Rose has termed 'fragmenting the social into a multitude of markets' (1999a: 146). But, as both these writers emphasise, what actually took place was a more complex and comprehensive restructuring than can be summed up in the misleadingly simple term 'marketisation'. The restructuring process involved, right across the public service sector, the creation of separate and semi-autonomous intermediary public service providers which were typically regulated by a combination of 'market forces' operating within quasi-markets and direct regulation usually by quangos. (The relationships post-1988 between various kinds of state schools, quangos such as OFSTED or the QCA, and central government may be taken as paradigmatic.) Rose, analysing these developments from the perspective of a focus on governmentality, has described this as involving an attempt 'to establish new distantiated relations of control between political centres of decision and "non-political" procedures, devices and apparatuses – such as schools, hospitals or firms – upon whose conduct they are dependent' (Rose 1993: 295). Freedland, whose work is discussed more fully in Chapter 3, similarly argues that the direct relationship between citizen and government characteristic of most forms of social democratic public service provision, was replaced by marketised forms of 'triangular public service relationships' which positioned citizens primarily as individualised consumers of locally delivered services, thereby weakening and marginalising the political relationship between citizens collectively and the state. Both analyses see citizens as repositioned in their relation to the state *via* their restructured relationship to state-provided services. In his words:

> The citizen, instead of being able to use the straight path to the government or central state, is re-routed round two sides of the institutional triangle. This triangularity is perfectly expressed when the government or one of its departments insists that it is not *directly responsible* for a particular kind of public service but only *indirectly accountable* for its due provision by the intermediate institution.
>
> (Freedland 2001: 103, italics in original)

It is worth pointing out, however, that many commentators have emphasised that these attempts to depoliticise public service delivery by distancing direct providers from government and emphasising ostensibly neutral market efficiency criteria, have been less than universally successful. Clarke *et al.*, analysing policies of the Thatcher era from the perspective of the 'managerialisation' of public services, have pointed out that:

> attempts to 'de-politicise' social policy by stressing the apparently ... neutral criteria of 'economy, efficiency and effectiveness' that are to be achieved by the new management, have only been partially successful. In a variety of areas – the NHS, the introduction of Community Care, the Poll Tax, education, law and order – the government has failed to devolve responsibility (and blame), being publicly and politically identified with (and blamed for) the new policies.
>
> (1994: 231)

This consideration brings us to a very brief discussion of the *identity* component of neo-liberal citizenship. The attempt to structure a new form of 'citizen' identity has had a twin focus. On the one hand, as the foregoing account suggests, strenuous efforts have been made to position and 'interpellate' citizens as *consumers,* whose main concern *vis-à-vis* the state is to individualistically obtain value-for-money and quality of service delivery for themselves and their dependants, and to seek remedies and compensation if services are inadequate. The underlying rhetorical appeal is to the idea of consumer sovereignty, even if this is severely qualified in practice.[4] The second focus of the new 'citizenship' identity centres on the idea of individual *enterprise*, which is also (and significantly) constructed primarily in marketised terms. Ideally, this new citizen is to be 'an entrepreneur of him or herself', an individual disposed 'to conduct his or her life, and that of his or her family, as a kind of enterprise, seeking to enhance and capitalize on existence itself through calculated acts and investments' (Rose 1999a: 164).[5]

1.3 Citizenship in Britain: an 'invisible' phenomenon with strong effects

As the discussion so far has suggested, citizenship in Britain presents something of a paradox. On the one hand there is no generally used vocabulary of citizenship; people do not for the most part think of themselves as citizens; citizenship education has been weak or absent; theoretical engagement with citizenship has been under-developed, at least until quite recently. In this sense, citizenship is close to having been 'invisible' for much of the postwar period and was perhaps even more so in the pre-war period. But, on the other hand, Britain was one of the pioneers of liberal social citizenship and carried it further than many other Western democracies (if less far than in Scandinavia). And since the late 1970s, a large part of what has been most vigorously contested in British politics has been, in effect, competing *models* of citizenship – as neo-liberal 'citizenship' has fought and partially displaced social citizenship (to an as yet uncertain extent). We shall suggest, therefore, that the most significant peculiarity of citizenship in Britain is that it has operated in many ways as an invisible phenomenon but a phenomenon with *strong effects*.[6]

A recent study, which is unusual in that it brings out with particular clarity the differential effects on political attitudes and identities of different forms of citizenship being more or less strongly institutionalised, is S. M. Lipset and G. Marks' (2000) study *It Didn't Happen Here*, subtitled 'Why Socialism Failed in the United States'. The essence of their argument is that the inability of socialists in the USA to establish a viable social democratic *party*, and the resulting chronic absence of a social democratic influence in government, are not only linked to higher levels of social inequality and poverty in the USA as compared with most European nations, but also correlates strongly with differences in *citizens' attitudes* about such matters as government responsibility for supporting the unemployed or those living in poverty. These writers provide evidence indicating, for example, that in nations with strong social democratic traditions, voters were very significantly more likely to agree with statements such as 'government should provide a decent standard of living for the unemployed' or 'government should provide everyone with a guaranteed basic income' than was the case in nations like the USA with a much weaker institutionalisation of social democracy (ibid.: 289). Commenting on the pivotal role of political parties in articulating and promoting what are in effect differing conceptions of citizenship and its associated rights, as well as their effectivity in shaping political identities, Lipset and Marks, in a key passage, argue that:

> In a democracy, political parties respond to issues citizens think are important ... But over the longer term, it makes sense to think that political parties shape preferences ... Political parties tie diverse issues together in coherent packages that can be more easily understood and acted upon ... There are several ways in which voters could conceive their territorial, ethnic, class, status and gender identities. Political parties bring some sources of identity to the foreground and leave others politically dormant. Finally, political parties influence legislation, and by doing so, leave a durable imprint on society.
>
> (ibid.: 278–9)

In addition to establishing these key general points, these writers go on to suggest that notwithstanding the reversals widely inflicted on social democracy in the 1980s and 1990s,

> [T]his does not mean that the history of social democracy makes little difference for current policy. Studies that find that social democratic participation in government has made little difference in the 1980s and 1990s also stress that *prior*

experience of social democracy remains a powerful factor shaping contemporary variations. This is because institutions, once created, can shape future change. Once a government policy is in place, it is likely to be defended by those who benefit from it. A policy legacy may also shape expectations about what government is able to do.

(ibid.: 287–8)

We shall return to some of these more specific and historically contingent matters in subsequent chapters.

1.4 Ways of thinking and living 'citizenship': the formation of political identities

It is now time to focus more closely upon the elusive issue of the ways in which ordinary citizens in the UK have conceptualised and experienced citizenship. An illuminating approach to this problem is suggested by the historian David Cannadine's (1998) treatment of the phenomenon of *class* in Britain. Cannadine does not dissent from the common perception that the British are preoccupied, even obsessed, with class. He suggests, however, that a key reason why this perennially fascinating phenomenon is so hard to pin down is that for generations, British people have actually operated with (and conceptualised their society in terms of) *three different* models of class, sometimes drawing upon more than one of these models at the same time, and often switching between them as circumstances change or as influential politicians have articulated particularly persuasive visions of 'class' and the relations between classes. The three models Cannadine identifies are, briefly: (i) class as an ordered hierarchy of rank or degree: a consensual status-order in which every individual has their place; (ii) class as a three-category model: 'above', 'middle', and 'below'; and (iii) a dichotomous model: 'them and us', the exploiters and the exploited, the patriotic majority against a decadent elite, etc. Our concern here is not to try to assess the validity of Cannadine's bold historical thesis but rather to follow his lead when he comes to discuss the relationship between language, social identities and these different models:

the *models* of British society are more important in the constitution of our social understandings and the construction of our social identities than the *language* in which they are expressed and articulated. For the language of ranks or of class cannot by itself create social descriptions or social identities, since it might be referring to any one of the three available models of society, and the language itself does not make clear which ... The connection between social vocabularies and social identities is more complex and contingent than is generally recognised. The 'language' of class is not the real issue: the real issue is the models of society which that and other languages articulate, make real and bring to life.

(ibid.: 166)

The case of citizenship is not, of course, perfectly analogous but the parallels are suggestive. One complication is that 'class' itself is strongly implicated in how Britons have thought about citizenship. Moreover, the principle of division (or at least separation) inherent in class seems, at first sight, to be opposed to the principle of universality that is formally inherent in citizenship. This is not as fundamental a problem as it might at first seem, however, for as Cannadine suggests, class in Britain has strongly to do with *totalising* conceptions of society and the relations between key groupings within society – and the case is similar for the different models of citizenship we have distinguished. Also, both sets of conceptions (class and citizenship) inevitably locate the *individual* in relation to such totalities (however conceived). Another key insight that can be drawn from Cannadine concerns the pivotal role played by political parties and especially by charismatic party leaders, in articulating novel ways of seeing 'how society is' and thereby actively constructing the relations between the groups which make up the society. Cannadine's views in this respect are remarkably similar to those of Lipset and Marks discussed above. British politicians, he suggests, have down the centuries, been involved in two kinds of inter-related activities:

The first consists of providing the collective social categories through which people can understand society as a whole. The second consists of trying to persuade them that they belong to one collective category, rather than another, by extolling the merits of one group, while denouncing the other group (or groups) as being wholly without virtue ... Thus regarded, the task of politicians is the creation and manipulation of social identities, sometimes articulated in the language of class, sometimes not. It is not so much that 'real' social identities directly inform and animate party politics; it is that party politics is concerned with creating social identities.

(ibid.: 169)

An interesting case in point is that of Margaret Thatcher, whose role in these respects is brilliantly analysed by Cannadine (ibid.: 171–80). Building on his discussion, it can be argued that during her premiership, Mrs Thatcher's political rhetoric – as well of course as a massive amount of relevant legislation (e.g. the sale of council houses, curtailing the powers and immunities of trade unions) – played a significant part in encouraging many British people to redefine their political and social identities in ways more consonant with neo-liberal conceptions of citizenship while weakening, though by no means destroying, their attachment to social citizenship. It is noteworthy that a key element of her rhetorical strategy was to publicly disavow the relevance of the *language* of class[7] while simultaneously pursuing policies which targeted organised labour, and in particular the miners (whom she *privately* saw as 'the crack division of the working class' who had to be defeated) (ibid.: 178). Cannadine suggests that like many successful populists before her, she skilfully constructed a series of *binary* categorisations of 'the British people' in which the language of class was conspicuous by its absence: for example, ordinary people as consumers versus self-serving and 'arrogant' state bureaucrats and professionals; or, the productive, hard-working majority versus 'parasites' sunk in 'dependency culture'. In such ways, Cannadine argues, 'she politicised social categories and social models in an adversarial way as no British political leader had done since Lloyd George' (ibid.: 179). How far she was successful in her radical ambition to 'change the way we look at things, to create a wholly new attitude of mind' (Thatcher 1989: 98) is, of course, debatable. But what is of most interest for our purposes is the insight that the *enterprise* of restructuring political identities and allegiance to different models of citizenship, can be carried out through vocabularies that refer explicitly neither to citizenship nor to class but imply both.

Having, hopefully, established these general points, we shall now examine in more detail the linguistic categories and social images which – as means of imagining political identities and senses of citizenship – seem to be most closely associated with the three main models of citizenship we have already distinguished: citizens-as-subjects, social citizenship, and consumer/entrepreneurial 'citizenship'. All three models, we suggest, are still 'in play', though the appeal of 'citizen-as-subject' is almost certainly diminishing and may be in terminal decline.

1.4.1 Citizens-as-subjects

For at least the last two decades it has probably been only in certain exceptional contexts that British citizens have expressed their sense of political identity through an *explicit* use of the language of being 'a subject'. An interesting case in point is provided by the following interview between Robert Coles, an American psychiatrist, and a 10-year-old child from a strongly 'loyalist' family in Northern Ireland in the early 1980s:

> A Protestant child in Belfast sitting under a portrait of Queen Elizabeth, told my wife and me that 'the Queen is our mother: she holds all her subjects together, my Granny says, and if you're not one of her subjects, you'll be a girl who has lost her mother, and that's the saddest girl in the world. So we have to stay part of Great Britain; it's our homeland, my Granny says'.
>
> (Coles 1986: 56)

Here we can glimpse how such forms of consciousness make sense and persist in the exceptional context of a Protestant Unionism which at this time saw itself as particularly under siege.

Such cases apart, however, the language of being a subject seems to have figured mainly as 'background' though also, of course, in ceremonial contexts. Until very recently, for example, UK passports continued to refer to their bearers as 'her Majesty's subjects'.[8] And yet, a sense of being a subject-citizen, part of a monarchical and imperial nation – a nation led (at least in good times) by those 'naturally fitted' to rule, has almost certainly been the axis of the political identity of a significant proportion and sometimes perhaps a majority of UK citizens. The construction of this identity has a very long history, and was a work of continuing endeavour and often of deliberate calculation. The connections between monarchy, empire, military and naval prowess, and a

sense of nationhood have been extensively examined by historians. Tom Nairn, for example, has seen the reconstitution of the
monarchy (and of the 'royal family') in the latter part of the
eighteenth century as being central to the construction of 'a
viable popular patriotism from which the dangerous acids of pop-
ulism and egalitarianism were bleached out' and a 'surrogate
national identity' created in which the Crown provided an indispensable symbolic focus for 'a national-popular identity com-
posed decisively "from above" ' (Nairn 1988: 136–7). The theme
of national identity is similarly stressed in Linda Colley's important series of studies of the forging of the nation in the critical
period 1707–1837 (see, for example, Colley 1986, 1996). Colley
points out how this formation of a distinctive British identity was
crucially dependent upon the deployment of a series of contrasts
with an array of imaginary 'others' who epitomised all that was *not*
part of this 'essential nationhood'. Of decisive importance here
was the project of cultivating identifications with the monarchy,
British naval and military victories, and (in some ways most
importantly) the British Empire. An extensive body of historical
and sociological research on school curricula and school textbooks in England and Wales has similarly highlighted the part
played by educational institutions in the shaping of forms of subjectivity which, paradoxically, combined a passive acceptance of a
'subject' status as British citizen with a calmly assured ethnocen-
tric sense of national superiority. Ahier, for example, has shown
how over many decades, elementary and primary school texts in
history and geography played their part in shaping this form of
national identity:

> ... regional geography ... both established a national confi-
> dence and at the same time, a set of assumptions about other
> races. It located 'them' firmly in their climates and in lands
> which inhibited their growth towards civilisation ... In the so-
> called 'hot lands' of the Caribbean and Africa, life was
> thought to be too easy, there being no necessity to work and
> save ...
>
> In the books there is a clear implication of a natural hier-
> archy by which the British were given their place in the world.
> It is a place that demands hard work and delayed gratification
> but offers superiority.
>
> (1988: 163–4)

Besides the theme of nationhood, inflected in these particular ways, a second main aspect of the identity of citizen-as-subject seems to be closely linked to certain ways of thinking about *class*. The model which Cannadine calls 'class as hierarchy' is centrally and indeed logically associated with the 'subject' model of citizenship. In its purest form, this model envisages society as an ordered hierarchy of rank, descending from monarchy and aristocracy, through lesser degrees of distinction to ordinary people and ultimately to those some would now call the socially excluded. All who are politically enfranchised may be citizens; but traditional forms of *in*equality and deference coexist with the equality which citizenship formally confers. Moreover, there is a strong sense of the inevitability of there being 'leaders' and 'led', and not infrequently, an idea of some groups being naturally fitted to lead by virtue of their ancestry and/or upbringing. The appeal of at least aspects of this model has proved highly durable. Cannadine argues, for example, that 'the honours system' was irresistible not only to Tory party leaders but also to *Labour* Prime Ministers even in the post-war period.

Near contemporaries of such Labour leaders were the 'eighty-eight working-class children' studied by the sociologists Brian Jackson and Dennis Marsden in the late 1950s (Jackson and Marsden [1962] 1966). All these children were born into working-class homes in Huddersfield and became, to varying degrees, socially mobile as a result of having been the first in their families to have attended grammar schools. Interestingly, the opening sentence of this research study reads: 'this book is about working-class children turning into middle-class citizens' (ibid.: 15). The rich interview data provides fascinating glimpses of the developing political consciousness of these future citizens, who, as pupils in their grammar schools, had for the most part enthusiastically embraced the role of 'orthodox pupils', typically becoming 'prefects and leaders of school society' (ibid.: 212). Such identification with the hierarchy of their schools was not infrequently translated in adulthood into a straightforwardly deferential stance: 'I once thought I was Labour … but these public school boys, they know what they're doing; they know what they're talking about and how the job ought to be done' (ibid.: 196). In other cases, attitudes came closer to grudging respect combined with a sense of insurmountable inferiority:

Perhaps I'm going to somebody's house and I've got to meet some new people. Perhaps I'll walk round twice before I go and knock on the front door. And all the time I'm saying to myself, 'if you were a public schoolboy you'd walk straight up there and you wouldn't worry'. It only dawned on me after I'd left university, the big difference education makes. It's very good this public school education, you can really go ahead – it's leadership they say, they can train you for leadership. I don't think I'll ever get that confidence. It's got to be done right back in the schools.

(ibid.: 203)

Given the preoccupation of this research with education, it is perhaps not surprising that this group of respondents so often referred to the public schools as a focus for their imagery of how society was ordered and led. But for our purposes, what is most significant is their view that this was how society *should* be led, and their tendency to see traditional forms of hierarchy as part of the inevitable order of things – in the words of one female respondent: 'I don't approve of scrapping the public schools; they're a very valuable tradition . . . you've got to have the public schools to provide the leaders' (ibid.: 203). Summarising this part of their study, Jackson and Marsden themselves commented wryly on 'a built-in impetus to the right' in their respondents, and they note that 'for the former working-class child, a high regard for the Conservative elite ("the cream", "these chaps from the public schools") outweighed feelings about "disloyalty" to their background' (ibid.: 198).

The declining significance of these inter-related ways of experiencing citizenship and class has been widely discussed. Cannadine, for example, claims that 'for all her attachment to traditional order and inequality, Thatcherism was a portent of the *end* of deference' (1998: 177). But he locates the key turning point much earlier, citing a key passage by Peregrine Worsthorne written in the aftermath of Suez, which examines the transformation in social outlooks associated with 'the end of empire' in the 1950s and 1960s:

a social system which seemed right and proper while it produced a nation capable of ruling the world will look very different when that nation is in decline; . . . everything about the

British class system begins to look foolish and tacky when related to a second class power on the decline.

(Worsthorne 1959)[9]

And yet decline is not death; the citizen-as-subject is still far from being a mere object of historical curiosity. Among the more than 200,000 people who queued for hours for the lying in state of Queen Elizabeth the Queen Mother at Westminster Hall in early April 2002 there were many self-proclaimed 'royalists', and one man, interviewed on the BBC Radio 4 *Five O'Clock* programme, probably spoke for many when he said 'she's been a wonderful mother of the nation and it's been worth every one of the hours we've queued'.

1.4.2 Social citizens

Strangely, the subjective correlates of social citizenship seem to be even more elusive than those of either of the other two models we are considering. This is odd for at least two reasons: first, social citizenship is closely tied to the post-war era of 'consensus politics' and on that ground alone might seem to have been both securely rooted and widely shared, and second, social citizenship was explicitly theorised *as such* by T. H. Marshall. There is also a well-founded scholarly consensus about the key economic, political and institutional conditions of existence of this form of citizenship in Britain. It is quite widely accepted that these included:

- the 'long boom' of uninterrupted economic growth, full employment and relatively low inflation in the major Western economies from the period of post-war reconstruction until the global oil crisis of the mid-1970s;
- the greatly increased role of the state in the economy: Keynesian demand management; nationalisation (sometimes of uncompetitive sectors of the economy); and corporatism as a mode of intervention in industrial relations and economic planning;
- the greatly expanded role of the state in the financing and provision of welfare:[10] in part a set of prophylactic strategies for anticipating and containing social ills and problems; in part a particular (and compulsory) set of mechanisms for insuring citizens against risk; in part an institutional expression of a

commitment to collective betterment through national provision of a widening range of services free at the point of consumption (though publicly financed from taxation and government borrowing);

- the associated growth of 'bureau-professional regimes' of administration and control within each major sector of welfare (health, education, social services, etc.), by 'experts' who were employees of the central or local state; and the associated 'construction of distinctive relations between the internal regimes of the state, forms of political representation and "citizens"' (Newman and Clarke 1994: 23);

- an underlying faith in 'environmental' explanations of 'the causes of personal success and failure ... linked to a certain positivism in the rationale of regulatory practices' (Rose 1999a: 133), and an associated faith in the statist forms of 'social engineering' associated with such theories.

Rather more controversially, one might add to this list Robert Reich's thesis that the capacity of nation–states and of business organisations in this period to shield their employees from the full rigours of international competition engendered a set of constraints which locked both workforces and management into a set of institutionalised arrangements which resulted in there being a *general* sharing in rising prosperity. This, he argues, resulted in part from the fact that under conditions of Fordist production in which 'the giant pyramid organisations at the core of each major industry co-ordinated their prices and investments', 'work stoppages posed such a threat to high-volume production that organised labour was able to exact an ever-larger premium for its co-operation' (Reich 1998: 162). The counterpart of this, however, was that there were related constraints on *management* to limit their own share of remuneration:

> it would be unseemly for executives who engaged in highly visible rounds of wage bargaining with labour unions, and who routinely responded to government requests to moderate prices, to take home wages and benefits widely in excess of what other Americans earned.

Also, within the framework of a national economy, production workers' wages 'could not be allowed to sink too low, lest there be insufficient purchasing power in the economy'. These conditions, Reich argues, rendered sufficiently plausible a rhetoric that:

> under the stewardship of the corporate statesman, no set of stakeholders – least of all white-collar executives – was to gain a disproportionately large share of benefits of corporate activity; nor was any stakeholder – especially the average worker – to be left with a share that was disproportionately small.
>
> (ibid.: 170)

This analysis suggests, of course, that even in a society lacking a strong social democratic tradition (Reich's analysis applies to the USA), powerful economic and political conditions in this period exerted pressures in the direction of *collective* betterment – at least in the economic sphere.

But, when we turn to consider the forms in which involvement with these institutional realities was thought and lived in Britain, we encounter nothing that is very sharply defined, least of all a vibrant tradition and vocabulary of common social citizenship. It may be that in contrast to the status of citizen-as-subject, social democratic citizenship never managed to find a potent symbolic focus. It may also be that insofar as it was the expression of a *compromise* – truly satisfactory neither to socialists and other radical egalitarians nor to aspiring individualists – it lacked the capacity to engender the commitment that is necessary for something to function as a strong basis of identity. Marshall himself, writing only four years after the end of the war, believed that certain kinds of common experiences which transcended class differences would be potent in generating a sense of shared citizenship. He thought it very important, for example, that there should be participation in a range of social rituals emphasising equality of status with fellow citizens:

> Even when benefits are paid in cash, ... class fusion is outwardly expressed in the new form of common experience. All learn what it means to have an insurance card that must be regularly stamped (by somebody), or to collect children's allowances or pensions from the post office.
>
> (Marshall and Bottomore 1992: 33)

Similarly, he argued that 'the common experience offered by a general health service embraces all but a small minority at the top and spreads across the important class barriers in the middle ranks of the hierarchy' (ibid.: 34). It may be, however, that such appeals to commonality had their greatest resonance in the aftermath of war and in a context where the injustices associated with social inequality were highly visible. It was, after all, in the context of both war and conspicuous inequality that Sir William Beveridge successfully appealed to the national imagination with his 'fantasy of a patriotic war against five oddly named giants: Want, Disease, Ignorance, Squalor and Idleness' – an appeal so successful that his report became an instant best-seller (Pimlott 1992).[11] Corroborative evidence for such an interpretation comes from some of the wartime surveys of public opinion conducted by Mass Observation. A study entitled *The Mood of Britain – 1938 and 1944* argued that the experience of 'total war' had substantially changed public attitudes:

> The 'selfish' set of attitudes revealed in pre-war studies gave way to a sense of purpose which went beyond self and immediate convenience. MO found the Beveridge Report had focused the national mood powerfully. From 1943 people began to show a willingness to itemise what was wrong with British society and to suggest ways of putting it right.[12]
>
> (Hennessy 1993: 78)

It is, of course, important not to exaggerate either the scope or depth of such solidaristic feelings engendered by wartime experiences. Resentment – against traditional class hierarchy and privilege – was a potent element in the aspiration to build a better and fairer world. Nevertheless, the circumstances of a national patriotic war did enable the cohesive effects of national-ethnic-military citizenship to link up with a set of aspirations for social justice and collective betterment under the aegis of the social state. Arguably, however, as Britain moved away from the experience of war and out of post-war austerity into a time of 'class-ridden property' (Halsey 1978), such social solidarity was increasingly fragmented – not only by older class antagonisms but also by new sources of division. Such sources included the increasingly instrumental aspirations and privatised lifestyles of 'affluent workers', as well as the economistic aims and tactics of the trade unions that represented them (Goldthorpe *et al.* 1968a, 1968b, 1969). Also significant, however, were divisions relating to social democracy itself. Certainly, by the late 1970s, social democracy was assailed (in theory and in practice) not only from the New Right but also from the radical Left – for its alleged elitism, non-accountability, and disconnectedness from 'grass-roots' concerns (CCCS 1981). By this stage, the hyphenated society of democratic-welfare-capitalism seemed to many people to have one hyphen too many – even if they could not agree which one it was!

It seems, then, that the sense of common social citizenship engendered by wartime conditions may have become increasingly difficult to sustain as economic and social conditions changed. This is not to say, however, that social citizenship as an institutional reality was fatally weakened. For one thing, key institutions of 'social democracy' – pensions, public schooling, progressive taxation – had their origins long before the Second World War. For another, the interlocking self-interest of the employees and the beneficiaries of welfare institutions protected a range of public services from a succession of assaults, for example by the radical free-marketeers of the Thatcher years – most evidently in the case of the National Health Service (cf. Lipset and Marks 2000). There also remains – albeit to a problematic degree – a shared sentiment that protection against some areas of risk may best be provided by public rather than private means. Nevertheless, from the late 1970s, a new basis of 'citizenship' was being actively constructed: as we have seen, the stage was being set for the appearance of the entrepreneurial/consumer citizen.

1.4.3 Entrepreneurial/consumer citizens

We have already discussed at some length the underlying structuring of this form of citizenship and the conditions under which it developed in the UK. In terms of political identities, however, once again, no confident or extensive vocabulary of neo-liberal citizenship developed – notwithstanding the potency of the underlying forces at work or the fact that determined efforts were made in the early 1990s to actively articulate conceptions of citizenship thought to be appropriate to a modern marketizing Conservatism. The most coherent and focused of these attempts was the Citizen's Charter campaign of the 1990s during John Major's first term as Prime Minister. The ideal citizen of the Citizen's Charter was unequivocally an individual who defined their 'citizenship' primarily in the form of enhanced consumer rights and one who had a legitimate expectation that it would be possible to *enforce* those rights through mechanisms that could prove effective against the 'producer interest' of allegedly recalcitrant state employees and institutions. In this sense, the Citizen's Charter was an adjunct to the Conservative policies of privatisation of state enterprises like railways, gas, electricity, water, and the creation of quasi-markets in areas like education and health. All this was made quite explicit in the rhetoric surrounding the launch of the initiative. An early document of the Citizen's Charter Unit stated: 'too often, public sector organisations seemed to deliver services that were designed to suit the providers rather than the recipients' (Citizen's Charter Unit 1992: 7), while Major himself forcefully declared: 'there must no longer be a hiding place for sloppy standards, lame excuses and attitudes that patronise the public' (John Major, cited in *The Independent*, 6 July 1991).

It is important to emphasise here that the Citizen's Charter sought to define and promote an alternative form of 'citizenship' rather than simply substituting consumerism for citizenship, as some critics have claimed. More was involved than the right to claim rebates when the trains ran late. The consumer rights that were enhanced were, at least in many instances, rights which had to be activated quasi-politically rather than through a straightforward market mechanism, for example, enhanced parental choice of schools. Other rights increased the accountability of state services directly to the users of those services, e.g. the right of parents to receive an annual report on their children's progress in school, or the requirement that OFSTED reports on school inspections should be published and available to parents and other interested parties. Such reforms were, indeed, intended to empower the 'customer' (at least within limits) but they operated through mechanisms of *political* empowerment. Of course, Citizen's Charter rights were often not reciprocal: the empowerment of citizen-consumers went hand in hand with the disempowerment of citizens as employees (at least in many sectors of state employment). Also, as Keith Faulks has noted, some groups of citizens were offered very minimal rights, for example, 'the Job Seeker's Charter promised only that people would be treated with courtesy' which was, Faulks suggests 'little compensation for a person struggling to survive and overcome a clerical mistake which delays his or her benefit' (1998: 139).

Nevertheless, it would be foolish to deny that many aspects of this agenda were popular and it is clear that they would be difficult to reverse radically.[13] The specific initiatives which clustered directly under the umbrella of the Citizen's Charter – the Parent's Charter, the Student's Charter, the Job Seeker's Charter and the rest were, as we have seen, but a small part of the much more extended and far-reaching sweep of neo-liberal structural reforms which together made 'consumer citizenship' so potent. Furthermore, there can be little doubt that New Labour in office has enthusiastically adopted and even intensified various aspects of the neo-liberal agenda of empowering consumers and promoting the values of enterprise. New Labour policy documents have reiterated the familiar narrative of the evils of 'producer self-interest' even while suggesting that the party's 'modernising' policies are steadily overcoming such obstacles to efficiency and accountability. The following passage from the 2001 Green Paper *Schools: Building on Success* exemplifies this:

> In the 20th century, the professional could often expect to be treated as an authority whose judgement would be rarely questioned and who was therefore rarely held to account; . . . particularly in the public sector, services were often arranged to suit the producer rather than the user.
>
> Teaching, by contrast, is in many ways a 21st century profession. More perhaps than any other, the teaching profession accepts accountability; . . . teachers know they are there to serve pupils and parents.
>
> (DFEE 2001 paras 5.4 and 5.5)

Not only this, but Tony Blair himself has famously complained about 'the scars on his back' resulting from his under-appreciated battles to further 'modernise' state services, allegedly in the teeth of 'reactionary' resistance from certain groups of state employees. And in the area which is the main focus of this book, the ostensibly access-widening promotion of 'life-long learning' by New Labour has in fact gone hand in hand with a clear policy shift, originated by the Tories, whereby students entering higher education are increasingly required to finance their higher education through student loans and other forms of private finance. In this and other areas, the invitation to 'invest in yourself' (often moralistically represented as both a public and personal 'duty'), could

indeed be interpreted as part of a process of shifting the dominant paradigm of citizenship in the direction of greater economic
individualism. Central aspects of the lives and opportunities of
young citizens are here being restructured: opportunities which a
previous generation could access as entitlements of citizenship
are now increasingly available only on terms which involve individualised and familial economic calculation and risk (or, in the
case of a favourably circumstanced minority, are things which can
be comfortably subsidised out of accumulated family assets, and
sometimes even further subsidised by sponsorship from future
employers).

But for all that, neither in the days of the Citizen's Charter nor
today in the second term of a New Labour government, does it
seem to be the case that people think about or talk about these
matters in terms of which suggest a confident and strongly articulated sense of being a new kind of citizen. Once again, the vocabulary of citizenship, even when directly promoted as it was in the
case of the Citizen's Charter, failed to resonate with contemporary political consciousness. The new rights have often been welcomed; their take-up has in some cases been enthusiastic but they
do not seem, to any extent, to have been consciously incorporated
into something experienced as a sense of changing *citizenship* –
whether enhanced or diminished.

Chapter 2

Prospects for social national citizenship in the United Kingdom

Imperilled but not impossible?

2.1 Introduction

In this chapter we examine a range of challenges faced by what we shall for the moment call 'social national' citizenship, and we go on to offer a tentative assessment of the prospects of sustaining this form of citizenship in contemporary Britain. Our review in Chapter 1 of the distinctive character of citizenship in Britain has implicitly recognised that citizenship is inherently *contested* – both as a concept and in terms of the historically specific forms in which it is institutionalised. No less an authority than Aristotle, in *The Politics*, recognised that citizenship is a matter about which 'there is no unanimity of agreement' (1981: 168). Moreover, the progressive establishment and extension of citizenship rights have, to a significant extent, been the product of religious, class, gender and ethnic contestation. And the extension of such rights in the future is unlikely to be conflict-free: as Ralph Dahrendorf has observed 'the class conflict for the extension of the entitlements of citizenship is the precondition for extending the range of those eligible for them' (1996: 35).

In spite of all this, we shall in the remainder of this book use the term citizenship – without further qualification – to designate that *form* of citizenship which both includes significant *social* elements as rights of citizenship and which is grounded in membership of a nation, hence our earlier formulation 'social national' citizenship. In so doing we are not, of course, making any claim that there exists a clearly articulated and vibrant *citizenship identity* of this kind in modern Britain. Chapter 1 has sufficiently explained why this is not the case. Nor are we denying the existence or the potency of past or competing conceptions of citizenship. However, in adopting and endorsing this conception of citizenship, we do contend that we are not simply arbitrarily privileging one definition of citizenship over others. Our use of citizenship broadly follows that of Marshall and is in some respects indebted to Heater's attempt to define and defend a 'holistic' *ideal* of citizenship (Heater 1990).[1] Heater puts very clearly the essence of the case for regarding a minimum set of social rights as indispensable to effective citizenship in modern nations:

> Without a certain minimum of education, standard of living and leisure time neither the aptitude for civic awareness nor the dignity of the egalitarian principle is possible. In a world of economic inequalities market forces alone cannot achieve these desiderata for all. Since citizenship is a right of the individual *vis-à-vis* the public realm, then the public realm ... must accept the responsibility for ensuring these minimal conditions of its exercise. What is more, the grounds must be clearly accepted as deriving not from charity or compassion, but from the rights and justice which accrue to the status of citizen.
>
> (ibid.: 335)

The reference in this passage to a certain measure of egalitarianism as the basis for dignity is closely linked to Marshall's key distinction between 'quantitative or economic inequality' and 'qualitative inequality'. For Marshall, the extension of citizenship to include a modicum of social entitlements was the key to establishing qualitative equality by making formal civic and political rights substantive for all citizens in a society where quantitative inequalities would persist and might even increase. As such, he argued, social citizenship had developed to become a key source of human dignity, a bastion of social solidarity, and also the basis of a free society in that, as Dahrendorf points out 'qualitative inequalities are incompatible with free societies' (1996: 41). We contend that forms of 'citizenship' which erode (or never conceded) social entitlements as rights of citizenship involve a diminution of the *principle* of citizenship; they are not simply alternative and equally valid types of citizenship. This applies particularly to neo-liberal 'citizenship', which we regard as a project aimed at undermining the fuller expression of the citizenship principle achieved in various Western Europe nations after the Second World War.[2]

The linking of citizenship with *nationality* is also neither uncontested nor unproblematic. In the modern world, it is not difficult to see why many people have reservations about emphasising national belonging as an element of citizenship. On the one hand, social national citizenship was, during much of the twentieth century, inseparable from a third element: social-national-*military* citizenship – which was, *inter alia*, the condition of recruiting conscript but also patriotic armed forces in two World Wars. In the British case this nation-military couple may been seen by some as not only distasteful in itself but also an uncomfortable reminder of a national colonial past about which many modern British citizens feel at best ambivalent. Especially in a world of 'democracy without enemies' (Beck, U. 1998) these associations can be experienced as both regrettable and anachronistic. Added to all this is the more recent experience of resurgent nationalism in areas such as the Balkans or Rwanda, which has created terrifying reminders of the ways in which strong national (and especially ethnic-national) identifications can assume pathological forms – displayed in such chilling practices as 'ethnic cleansing'. It has to be acknowledged therefore that a focus on nationality can appear backward-looking, exclusive, and in some cases as verging on being racist. Such concerns can, moreover, be reinforced from other directions, for example, by those whose visions of the future – post-modern, late-modern, post-industrial, etc. – imagine a world in which separate nations have become obsolescent and where we are invited to see ourselves as 'world citizens' or, more atomistically, as mobile entrepreneurial individuals, unencumbered by anachronistic allegiances to nation or territory, free to carve out our own futures in a brave new globalising world (Reich 1991, 1998).

In spite of all these understandable and influential reservations, we contend that nationality will continue to be essential to sustaining viable forms of citizenship for some considerable time to come. The essential arguments supporting this view have been cogently set out by the political theorist David Miller. It is worth quoting him at some length because he articulates precisely the link between nationality, social solidarity and citizenship which we are endorsing:

> I want to argue that nationality answers one of the most pressing needs of the modern world, namely how to maintain

solidarity among the populations of states that are large and anonymous, such that citizens cannot possibly enjoy the kind of community that relies on kinship or face-to-face interaction ... I assume that in societies in which economic markets play a central role, there is a strong tendency towards social atomisation, where each person looks out for the interests of herself and her immediate social network. As a result it is potentially difficult to mobilise people to provide collective goods, it is difficult to get them to agree to practices of redistribution from which they are not likely personally to benefit, and so forth. These problems can be avoided only where there exists large-scale solidarity, such that people feel themselves to be members of an overarching community, and to have social duties to act for the common good of that community ... Nationality is *de facto* the main source of such solidarity.

(Miller 2000b: 31–2)

It is essential to note, however, that Miller goes on to distance his conception of nationality and national identity from 'conservatism of the Oakeshott-Kedourie-Minogue variety' (ibid.: 33), arguing that in modern liberal democracies, nationality implies neither a requirement for narrow cultural closure nor for some strong form of 'communitarian' value consensus. We must, he declares, 'hold on to the principle of nationality, while striving to forge national identities that can accommodate the pluralism and mutability of contemporary culture' (Miller 1995a: 420). Nevertheless, he insists, nations do remain in a certain crucial sense 'communities', albeit partially imaginary communities: 'nations are not voluntary associations, but communities within which most members are born, live and die, so that we are bound together with our compatriots in a *community of fate*' (ibid.: 416, our italics). And within the foreseeable future, despite the impact of globalisation, it is not easy to identify any alternative basis for this kind of extended community other than that of nation. (We shall examine certain aspects of the debate about globalisation in Chapter 3.) Nationality, then, seems to be the only viable focus for attachments to citizenship; while, for the foreseeable future, it is likely to remain the case that the majority of *rights* of citizenship will continue to be based upon nationality. Moreover, attempts to protect and extend human rights more widely are also likely to chiefly take the form of initiatives by nation–states – albeit with the important catalyst of pressures from key NGOs and other lobbying organisations. To recognise all this, however, is not to say that the task of sustaining such attachments will be easy, nor should we under-estimate the potency of various forces now threatening citizenship.

2.2 Some challenges to social national citizenship

There are perhaps three major developments which pose a serious threat to citizenship in modern Britain. These are, first, the direct threat of attempts to promote neo-liberal 'citizenship'; second, the significance of increasing affluence, privatised lifestyles, and consumerism; and third, and ironically, the danger that citizenship will be dissipated by the proliferation of a host of *new* citizenship agendas that threaten to obscure the core focus on the shared rights and responsibilities of social national citizenship. We have already discussed the impact of neo-liberal 'citizenship' at some length. Here, we shall focus on the second and third of our three challenges.

2.2.1 Affluence, privatised life-styles, privatisation and consumerism

As long ago as the mid-1960s, Goldthorpe and Lockwood's classic 'affluent worker' studies drew attention to the association between rising affluence and a tendency for British families to turn inward and become increasingly preoccupied with consumption-oriented 'privatised' lifestyles (Goldthorpe *et al.* 1968a, 1968b, 1969). Wholesale *embourgeoisement* was shown *not* to be occurring, especially in the 'relational' and political arenas. But the studies did point strongly to the increased importance of family-centred consumption in the lives of this group of relatively affluent manual workers. (The research also identified very similar trends in the 'control group' sample of lower middle-class workers.) Two decades later, Margaret Thatcher's stratagem of selling council houses to their tenants brilliantly capitalised on this same preoccupation with privatised self-betterment among the British working classes – creating the basis for what was proclaimed to be a new kind of 'property-owning democracy'. And this was of course but one of a whole raft of Tory privatisation measures which successfully appealed to the self-interest of better-off citizens. More recently, the continuing rise in the economic well-being of the majority of the population, albeit in a context of widening overall inequality, as well as the spectacular rises in property values in the mid-1980s and at the turn of the century, may well have operated to further detach the better off from a sense of obligation to those less fortunately circumstanced, and to have reinforced self-regarding economic individualism. Such moves have, of course, been reinforced by active efforts on the part of both Conservative and New Labour governments as well as the financial services industry to convince 'consumer-citizens' that they *all* now have the capacity, the freedom and indeed the duty to make *private* provision for themselves and their own futures. In these senses, it seems, privatisation begat privatised orientations begat privatisation.

Consumption, of course, is not only an economic matter; it also has a very significant symbolic component – and this is closely linked to a further meaning of the term 'privatisation'. The post-modernist sociologist Zygmut Bauman has argued that in the past forty years or so, choice itself has been privatised – and in a double sense. Not only has there been a 'hyping' of consumer choice as a dimension of identity formation and self-actualisation but commodification has been extended further and further across the *cultural* sphere – leaving, according to Bauman, almost no area in which non-commodified standards of judgement (or standards appealing to intrinsic worth) can hope to remain authoritative. This has, he suggests, created a radical reductivism in the sphere of values:

> Choice has been *privatised* – made into an attribute of individual freedom and identity-building. The promotion of any particular cultural pattern as essentially better than, or in any way 'superior' to, other available or conceivable choices, has been widely castigated and disdainfully rejected as an act of oppression.
>
> (Bauman 1995: 238, italics in the original)

An important implication of this is that *any* set of values, no matter how philistine or how amoral, may increasingly claim to be on a par with both educated standards of cultural judgement and ethically grounded values of social responsibility. In these respects, then, the erosion of deference as well as the relativising tendencies of a postmodern outlook, join together with triumphalist consumerism in a heady and destabilising mix whose overall effect may be to undermine collectivist values of many important kinds. Hebdidge has similarly suggested that

> from spiralling prices on the international art market ... and the role of PR in hyping everything from global brands to green issues and government policies, all the evidence points to the collapse of any firm line between 'culture' and 'commerce'.
>
> (1990: 19)

A related danger (for citizenship) is that for growing numbers of individuals, consumer identities may have become both more meaningful and may be experienced as more liberating than identities as either a producer or a citizen. Mark Poster argues that TV advertising is one source through which older and formerly 'hegemonic forms of self-constitution' may be shed, allowing viewers/consumers to reflexively 'regard their own subjectivity as a constituted structure, to regard themselves as members of a community of self-constitutors' (1990: 68). Many postmodernist writers have, of course, variously warned against or celebrated the supposed combined effects of 'the information society', the increased rapidity of circulation of advertising and other media images, the 'targeting' of media messages to niche audiences, etc. Some see this apocalyptically as rendering contemporary experience 'depthless' in the sense that 'there is nothing credible beneath or beyond the flat landscape of endless signification' (Slater 1997: 197), conditions which can be seen as productive of Jameson's famous spectre of the schizoid postmodern subject who lacks any stable sense of self or identity (Jameson 1984). It is not, of course, necessary to go this far to nevertheless recognise the important element of truth in Bryan Turner's vision of an increasingly fragmented consumer culture, generating at least in some instances, 'a fragmentation of sensibilities, a mixing of lifestyles and the erosion of any sense of a cogent political project or coherent political programme' (1989: 212). David Miller has similarly warned that those concerned with the preservation of citizenship should under-estimate neither 'the massive influence of consumption upon the political economy' nor 'the political economy inscribed in the historical projects given to people as consumers' (1995b: 55).

Perhaps the most insidious danger, however, lies not in the fragmentation of subjectivities which so preoccupies certain post-modernists but in the ways in which rising affluence has become increasingly linked to a growing absorption with individual and familistic success of a *positional* kind – a concern to have more and to do better than others. If this is so, it is, of course, not a new development at all – except perhaps in its scale and scope. But that may be the point! Such developments are perhaps most strik-ingly symbolised in what have been called 'winner-takes-all markets' (Frank and Cook 1996). Will Hutton has described the phenomenon as follows:

> Top performers in professions as disparate as the law and football, hospital surgery and investment banking are earning even higher salaries in relation to the average. More and more high-quality people are flocking to these sectors, however poor their prospects of reaching the summit, because the indifferent odds are more than compensated for by the exceptional rewards.
>
> (1997: 34)

Hutton goes on to note that the widening pay gap between these occupations/sectors and less glamorous possibilities elsewhere may be leaching talent away not merely from public sector occu-pations but also from less well rewarded though economically more productive fields such as engineering. This could easily con-tribute to a state of affairs in which careers in the public sector, particularly in welfare, education, and even the civil service, come to be regarded by increasing numbers of graduates as not merely second best but as a kind of permanent poor relation, attractive only to people who 'can't make it' in 'the real world' or whose 'do-gooding' motives are regarded as suspect and/or anachronistic.

The key associated danger is that of tax resistance. The affluent minority (for that is what they still are) may increasingly figure as a key point of reference for a perception that it is politically impossible to raise taxes, especially income and property taxes, and that policies of redistribution do not merely 'cripple' initi-ative and enterprise but are somehow permanently incompatible

with the needs of a modern, successful economy. The conjuring
up of the imagery of a 'tax revolt' has become an almost auto-
matic reflex in sections of the right-wing media whenever anyone
has the temerity to suggest that UK taxes might have to rise in
order to pay for improved public services. A recent illustration was
Daily Telegraph columnist Janet Daley's instant reaction to a suggestion by Matthew Taylor, director of IPPR,[3] that 'for social
democrats the good society is characterised not only by high
standards of public provision and the alleviation of poverty but
also a collective commitment to progressive taxation' (Taylor
2001). Daley's riposte, under the headline 'The road to Labour
Utopia is paved with taxpayers' money', gleefully attacked the
'jolly target' Taylor had provided in daring to suggest that it
might be possible to generate a broadly based positive commitment to progressive taxation. Scathingly, she characterises
Taylor's vision as: 'we do not want simply to confiscate as much
wealth as we need to run those bits of life that government ought
to organise ... we want you to enjoy paying tax for its own sake!'
(Daley 2001). Tellingly and symptomatically, she follows this by
setting up a dichotomous vision of society which sharply polarises
responsible caring *families* against the bureaucratic arrogant *state*:

> Margaret Thatcher was notoriously traduced for saying 'there
> is no such thing as society' when what she meant was that
> society consisted of the sum of its smaller parts like families
> and neighbourhoods. There is no ambiguity about what Mr.
> Taylor (and New Labour?) thinks is the essence of 'society': it
> is the state.

Taylor's own discussion in fact gives the lie to Daley's delibera-
tively mischievous suggestion that New Labour may also be 'con-
taminated' by such heresy:

> Tax is not a necessary evil but an expression of social soli-
> darity. In a world where we were free to talk about political
> destinations, this would surely unite New Labour zealots and
> traditionalists alike. But lack of vision and fear of a tax revolt
> mean that rather than advocating such a good society, Labour
> pretends we can have the spending without the commitment
> to pay for it.
>
> (Taylor 2001)

Alongside all this increasingly widespread negativity, the growing relative impoverishment of public sector provision – epitomised in lengthening waiting times for NHS treatment, sordid and even insanitary hospital wards, over-crowded classrooms, etc. – may powerfully add to the 'poor relation' perception of public service, whether as a place to pursue a career or as an unfortunate destiny that awaits those who are unable to 'provide for themselves'. Ironically, *not* having private health insurance could increasingly become a key signifier of being a 'second-class citizen' – at least for those in work.[4]

In sum, although it would be an error to regard the combination of rising affluence, privatisation in all its different meanings, and consumerism as the basis of a new 'master identity' (Isin and Wood 1999: 155), it would clearly be no less of a mistake to under-estimate the insidious appeal of these developments – which appear, albeit speciously, to offer an escape not only from 'oppressive' moral 'dogmatism' and cultural 'elitism', but also from forms of welfarism which can be denigrated as second-class and choice-denying.

2.2.2 The inflation of the citizenship agenda

An important consequence of the recent world-wide resurgence of interest in citizenship which we noted in Chapter 1 has been a proliferation of efforts to enlarge and/or re-focus citizenship so as to incorporate an array of *new* citizenship agendas. Although many aspects of these developments are both laudable and progressive, they may, nevertheless, have the unintended consequence of making the task of defending social national citizenship even more difficult than it already is – given the potency of the neo-liberal onslaught. Derek Heater, writing in 1990, presciently identified this risk:

> Citizenship as a useful political concept is in danger of being torn asunder; and any hope of a coherent civic education left in tatters as a consequence. By a bitter twist of historical fate, the concept, which evolved to provide a sense of identity and community, is on the verge of becoming a source of communal dissension. As more and more diverse interests identify particular elements for their doctrinal and practical needs, so the component parts of the citizenship agenda are being

made to do service for the whole. And under the strain of
these centrifugal forces, citizenship as a total ideal may be
threatened with disintegration.

(1990: 282)

There seem to be two fundamental and inter-related problems.
One is that a multitude of sectional interest groups will seek to
prioritise their particularistic agendas within the wider effort to
promote citizenship and citizenship education. The second is that
insofar as this becomes a general tendency, struggles *between* citizens over the meaning and application of citizenship may undermine the universalism which is indispensable if citizenship is to be
an effective force for progress and cohesion. Both of these tendencies are closely linked to the growth of 'identity politics', the
ever-widening claims on behalf of the 'politics of recognition',
and the clamour of 'voice' discourse (Moore and Muller 1999). As
an illustration of the diversity of citizenship agendas that now
exist, Isin and Wood's outstanding recent book *Citizenship and
Identity* (1999) contains discussions of the following: diasporic and
aboriginal citizenship including post-colonial identities; a diversity
of competing feminist challenges to conventional liberal citizenship; claims on citizenship in relation to gay and lesbian
rights; urban citizenship, technological citizenship and ecological
citizenship; cosmopolitan and global citizenship; cultural citizenship and the relationship of consumerism to citizenship – all
in addition to an opening section on civil, political and social citizenship. We are not, of course, suggesting that these issues are
unconnected with citizenship nor that any of them could or
should be wished away. However, as Isin and Wood themselves
remark: 'while sympathetic to the expressed need for a deep and
multi-layered conception of citizenship, we hope that the political
and theoretical difficulties of such a conception have become
apparent throughout this book' (ibid.: 153). Small wonder that
Heater was prompted to reflect in relation to his own attempt to
formulate an ideal of citizenship that 'maybe the attempt we are
making ... to bundle so much meaning into the term (citizenship) is unrealistically to overload its capacity' (1990: 282).

Quite clearly it will not be possible here to even begin to
address this complex array of specific issues. We shall instead
confine ourselves to a few remarks about the politics of recognition since the fate of this idea is illustrative of the core problem

we are trying to analyse. In its original formulation by the philosopher Charles Taylor, this concept was both carefully circumscribed and tentative (Taylor 1992). First, Taylor emphasised that a defensible politics of recognition should involve 'a presumption ... that all human cultures that have animated whole societies over some considerable stretch of time have something important to say to all human beings' (ibid.: 66). Second, he was at pains to stress that such a presumption was 'by no means unproblematic' and he continued:

> when I call this a 'presumption', I mean that it is a starting hypothesis with which we ought to approach the study of any other culture. The validity of the claim has to be demonstrated concretely, in the actual study of the culture.
>
> (ibid.: 65–6)

Even more unambiguously, he went on to insist that 'it can't make sense that as a matter of *right* we come up with a final concluding judgement that their value is great, or equal to others; ... the judgement ... cannot be dictated by a principle of *ethics*' (ibid.: 68–9, our italics). However, this is too often what has happened to the idea of recognition as it has increasingly become attached to identity. More and more commonly, not only are claims to recognition made on behalf of values and/or identities that are often quite minor elements of whole cultures (gay and lesbian rights, specific religious communities, enthusiasts for hunting), but it is also the case that such claims are now very commonly expressed as *demands* that full and equal respect be accorded to these identities by all citizens.[5]

There are two essential difficulties here: the problem of incoherence and the undesirable consequences that are likely to follow if such demands are pressed extensively. The incoherence problem itself has two main strands. One is highlighted by Taylor himself. It simply makes no sense to demand as a matter of *right* that others accord equal respect to views or practices which they sincerely find unpalatable, obnoxious or even just plain misguided! One of the merits of Rawls' distinction between the public sphere and the non-public sphere (Rawls 1993, 1999) is that it makes more limited demands in this regard. Citizens are required to support the right of others to live their lives in accordance with their own comprehensive theories of the good life (so long as these do not infringe the shared values of the public sphere); citizens are *not* required to *endorse* these diverse comprehensive theories. The second kind of incoherence concerns certain sorts of 'voice' discourse which underpin many contemporary demands for 'recognition'. Moore and Muller characterise the rise of 'voice' discourse as an often genuinely progressive development which has enabled 'a succession of previously marginalised, excluded and oppressed groups to enter the central stage, their histories to be recovered and their "voices" joined freely and equally with those already there' (1999: 191). However, they point out, what many of these voices are demanding is two kinds of recognition: not merely the right to be listened to respectfully but the further and more problematic claim to equal or in some cases superior epistemological validity in relation to previously 'dominant' and 'conservative' forms of knowledge. The kind of incoherence that can be involved here is, of course, that associated with thorough-going relativism. Claims to possession of valid knowledge tend to be assessed, Moore and Muller argue, not primarily by reference to reason, evidence and explicit methodological procedures but by privileging the social position from which the speaker speaks: 'this discourse warrants itself through assertions of naturalistic authenticity; it counters "hegemonic" epistemological knowledge claims with representations of the experience of exclusion attributed to those silenced by its dominance' (ibid.: 194). This can be both a shaky and sometimes a provocative basis from which to promote claims for recognition.

The vigorous public advocacy of recognition claims by diverse groups with differing and in some respects incompatible values and beliefs is also problematic in that it can lead to a polarisation of positions rather than the harmonisation which advocates of recognition avowedly seek. An illuminating if depressing case study of a process of this kind is Jasmin Zine's recent account of disputes among minority groups surrounding an anti-racist policy initiative issued by the Toronto District School Board in Canada. Zine summarises developments following the release by the Board, in November 1998, of 'a draft policy on anti-racism and ethno-cultural equity in education':

> A competing policy document challenging the specific focus on race, ethnicity and faith communities as being 'too narrow' argued that the notion of equity should be broadly

construed to accommodate the categories of other 'historically disadvantaged groups', such as women, the disabled, and
gays and lesbians, under a single comprehensive policy. A
debate over the implications of broad-based equity has
polarised communities along racial, ethnic and religious
lines. Religious and ethnic communities objected to the dis-
placement of race, ethnicity and religion and what they
regarded as the centring of sexual orientation in a policy
which would integrate gay and lesbian issues into the curriculum. Advocates for separate policies argued that all forms of
difference could not be equated and should be dealt with sep-
arately in terms of policy and practice.

(Zine 2001: 239)

While the politics of recognition is not the explicit focus of Zine's
account, the rich ethnographic data she provides clearly show
that competing demands for equal recognition of minority identities lay at the centre of some of the most intractable problems in
these debates. At one point, for example, she notes that 'critics of
the anti-racism and ethno-cultural policy felt strongly that the lack
of recognition of other marginalised groups in the policy was
completely unresponsive to the reality of many students in the
school system', and she cites a published response by Giese who
argued that

under the proposed guidelines, a female Jewish student will
have her identity as a Jew affirmed but not as a female ... a
gay immigrant student will have access to resources helping
him with language skills, but no place to turn for support with
coming out.

(Giese 1999, in Zine 2001: 255)

Recognition of gay and lesbian identities proved especially con-
tentious, with several representatives of ethnic and religious
groups construing 'racial' and religious identities as of a qualita-
tively different order of significance from what they labelled mere
'lifestyle' issues: the following comment by a representative of the
Muslim community is illustrative: 'we are dealing here with deep-
seated spiritual issues which form the core of our very existence,
and therefore there is no compromise when it comes to lifestyle
issues' (in Zine 2001: 262).

2.3 Some grounds for qualified optimism about the prospects for social national citizenship in Britain

The challenges to citizenship discussed in the previous section are formidable, especially when taken in conjunction with continuing efforts backed by extremely powerful forces to promote neo-liberalism, the values of shareholder capitalism, and so on. Despite this, however, there *are* also indications that these and other forces promoting economic individualism are not carrying all before them. It is, for example, arguable that even John Major's introduction of the avowedly neo-liberal Citizen's Charter in 1991, marked a retreat from what Neal Ascherson called 'high Thatcherism', insofar as it treated public services 'as something permanent which must be improved rather than as something abhorrent which must be dismantled' (Ascherson 1991). And even before this, *during* the days of high Thatcherism and not long after the 'Lawson boom' of the mid-1980s, some within the Conservative Party had become more than a little concerned that the promotion of unbridled self-interest had gone too far and was becoming politically damaging. One example was the campaign mounted in the late 1980s led by Tory minister Douglas Hurd to try to offset the growing public perception that Thatcherism had engendered a climate of individual and corporate greed exempli-fied by the figure of the 'loadsamoney yuppie' – the new rich apparently caring little for either civic virtue or the well-being of their fellow citizens (Beck, J. 1998: 127–9). In this context, a care-fully crafted version of the idea of 'the active citizen' was pro-moted as 'a necessary complement to that of enterprise culture' on the grounds that whereas 'public service may once have been the duty of an elite . . . today it is the responsibility of all who have the time and money to spare' (Hurd 1989). Hurd drew skilfully on older traditions of Conservatism, conjuring up Burkean images of 'small platoons' and the value of making voluntary con-tributions within a revivified sphere of civil society – all in an effort to stitch back together the diverging neo-conservative and neo-liberal tendencies within the party:

> The Conservative Party is moving forward from its justified concern with the motor of wealth creation towards a redefini-tion of how the individual citizen, business, or voluntary

group can use resources and leisure to help the community
... Underpinning our social policy are three traditions – the
diffusion of power, civic obligation, and voluntary service –
which are central to Conservative philosophy, and rooted in
British (particularly English) history ... The strongest loyal-
ties are to family, neighbourhood, and nation said Burke: 'to
love the little platoon we belong to in society is the first principle (the germ as it were) of public affections'.

(Hurd 1988)

Kenneth Baker, the then Secretary of State for Education, was
blunter and more succinct. In a speech to the Bow Group he
declared: 'there is another side to economic individualism; those
who succeed have obligations over and beyond that of celebrating
their own success' (*Daily Telegraph*, 28 April 1989). Despite such
advocacy, however, these attempts to moralise enterprise culture
proved less than persuasive, not least to the constituency to whom
they were most directly addressed. The contradictions within the
message were, at least at that time, perhaps too blatant to carry
much conviction.

Similarly, whether New Labour's much trumpeted vision of a
'Third Way' in politics really signals a major departure from the
dominance of neo-liberalism is, we believe, open to question. The
idea of the Third Way has, of course, been widely publicised, both
in academic writing (e.g. Giddens 1998, 2000a, 2000b) and in the
speeches of leading New Labour figures (e.g. Blair 1996; Straw
1998). We have, however, already noted some of the ways in
which certain of New Labour's actual policies display very strong
continuities with Tory initiatives grounded in economic individualism and the promotion of enterprise culture, even when they
are represented as elements of a more socially responsible agenda
oriented to widening access and opportunity. A key part of the
Third Way vision is that of a reinvigorated 'civil society' as a
sphere of voluntary and community action – partly to supplement
but also partly to replace the 'passivity' allegedly induced by state-
provided services. Such forms of 'active citizenship' have been
advocated as a way of combating dependency culture as well as
supposedly demonstrating the moral superiority of the Third Way
agenda over the 'naked' self-interest of 'pure' neo-liberalism. Jack
Straw, for example, in a speech on the Third Way delivered in
1998, declared:

In many ways the most important example of our approach is our commitment greatly to extend the idea and practice of volunteering – of people doing something for each other *rather than having the State do it for them and so diminishing them.* We have described this voluntary activity as the essential act of citizenship . . . are trying to develop the concept of 'the Active Community' in which the commitment of the individual is backed by the duty of all organisations – in the public sector, the private sector and the voluntary sector – to work towards a community of mutual care and a balance of rights and responsibilities.

(Straw 1998: para. 64–5, cited in Rose 1999b: 485–6, our italics)

As we have indicated, however, all this is strikingly redolent of Douglas Hurd's essentially rhetorical interventions a decade earlier. Similarly, Tony Giddens' recent exhortation to economic elites to exercise greater civic responsibility, uncannily echoes Kenneth Baker's admonishment of the self-indulgent 'yuppies' of the 1980s:

obligation and commitment go well beyond fiscal responsibilities. Those moralists who make extensive civic demands upon welfare recipients would do well to make them also of business leaders and other elite groups. A social contract of mutual obligation . . . must stretch from bottom to top.

(Giddens 2000a: 119)

The similarity between New Labour's approach and that of neo-conservative Tories goes significantly deeper than shared rhetoric, however. For both, there is a strong disposition to regard the substitution of voluntary activity for state-provided services within 'civil society' (what Alexander calls the 'informal non-state') as both a political and an ethical *advance* (Alexander 1995: 34). Now, we do not doubt that there may be many instances where such agencies have a valuable role to play, but we are concerned that here as elsewhere in New Labour's repertoire, there tends increasingly to be a dogmatic insistence that the private sector and the contributions of independent not-for-profit organisations, must *in principle* be preferable to provision by the state. The clear risk is that this project of redefining 'community' as a congeries of voluntary organisations and activities within a reinvigorated 'civil society' may insidiously erode an ever-widening range of citizenship *entitlements*. Heater's words quoted earlier are apposite: 'the grounds (on which a minimum of social benefits are provided) must be clearly accepted as deriving not from charity or compassion, but from the rights and justice which accrue to the status of citizen' (1990: 335).

It is, moreover, not only New Labour's critics on the Left who have detected a strand of disingenuousness in these efforts to present the party as capable of combining support for strongly neo-liberal economic policies with the regeneration of a strong commitment to a revived citizenship agenda. The neo-conservative philosopher Roger Scruton has highlighted what he sees as clear parallels between Thatcherism and the practice of New Labour in office. Reminding his readers that *out* of office, New Labour spokesmen repeatedly castigated 'the "culture of greed" which ... they associated with big business, with the city, with free trade and free markets', Scruton argues that *in* office and under Tony Blair:

> business is still firmly in the driving seat. The Prime Minister appoints business moguls to the House of Lords with the same unconscionable enthusiasm as Margaret Thatcher ... Look at Labour policy in any of the areas in which the capitalist giants have an interest – Europe, EMU, mergers and monopolies, the environment, agri-business – and you will see electoral promises and moral convictions crumbling before the imperatives of trade. The argument has been accepted, as it was accepted under Thatcher, that prosperity means growth, that growth means globalisation, and that globalisation means the abolition of local restraints ... Mr. Blair describes himself as a Christian Socialist: he is no such thing. Like Baroness Thatcher, he is a nineteenth century liberal. He may never have said 'you can't buck the market' but he acts as if it were true.
>
> (Scruton 1998)

Despite all this, however, two aspects of these developments may still offer some limited comfort to those who wish to see citizenship not merely preserved but strengthened. The first is that the voices of the critics of the dominance of self-interest and economic liberalism have not by any means been silenced. Albeit from a variety of very different political and philosophical positions, trenchant criticisms of the bankruptcy of economic individualism and morally unregulated capitalism have continued to be expressed. Scruton actually enlists Marx and Engels in developing his critique of unrestrained market forces:

> The failure of socialism does not let capitalism off the hook. There is something wrong with a society that is governed entirely by the imperatives of business, which recognises no restraint on trade apart from the market, and which makes business and enterprise into its primary values. When Marx and Engels wrote the *Communist Manifesto* they did not condemn capitalism for its economic power. They condemned it for its human cost. 'It has left no other nexus between man and man,' they wrote, 'than callous "cash payment" . . . It has resolved personal worth into exchange value'.
>
> (ibid.)

Such criticisms from such sources perhaps suggest the possibility of sustaining at least a broader community of interest (if not viable political alliances) among those who genuinely share a *moral* critique of neo-liberal 'citizenship'. A second source of optimism, albeit highly qualified, may be that the Third Way vision – for all its rhetoric and despite its obvious potential to facilitate misrecognition of New Labour's underlying policy thrust – is nevertheless a position which logically acknowledges the claims of citizenship at least to some extent: it represents itself, after all, as a position between the Scylla of corporatist bureaucratic welfarism and the Charybdis of 'discredited' neo-liberalism and naked economic individualism.

When we turn to consider the question of *nationality* and its implications for sustaining or reviving citizenship in the UK, there may be, at least in limited respects, rather stronger grounds for optimism. Recently, a number of influential commentators and groups have distanced themselves from those positions which seek to radically minimise the importance of nation–states and nationality in the modern world. It is, for example, significant that even very strong supporters of globalisation arguments do not all regard it as extinguishing either the role of nation–states or as necessarily diminishing the significance of nationality as a basis of identity. Thus Anthony Giddens rejects the claims of writers like Ohmae (1995) that nation–states are becoming a fiction, arguing instead that while globalisation may indeed remove some of their powers, nation–states will remain significant actors in many key contexts for the foreseeable future and that globalisation may in some cases actually strengthen national sentiments and aspirations:

> the recent upsurge in Scottish nationalism in the UK shouldn't be seen as an isolated example; it is a response to the same structural processes at work elsewhere, such as those in Quebec or Catalonia. Local nationalisms aren't inevitably fragmenting. Quebec may opt out of Canada as Scotland may opt out of the UK. Alternatively, each may follow the Catalan route, remaining quasi-autonomous parts of a wider national entity.
>
> (Giddens 1998: 31–2)

David Miller stresses the idea of what he terms 'nested national identities' as a basis for developing forms of national identification which are neither narrowly communitarian nor culturally exclusionary, arguing that we may actually need to become more rather than less self-conscious about national identity if we are to create a positive acceptance of the idea that 'people can identify equally strongly with a larger nation state and with a smaller national community inside it' (Miller 2000a: 31). The authors of the recent Parekh Report extend this idea of nested identities a stage further – to include not only national but also 'community' identities – holding out a vision of a Britain which is 'certainly "One Nation" but understood as a community of communities and a community of citizens' (Runnymede Trust 2000: 56). Miller, in a critique of strong 'politics of difference' arguments put forward by writers like Iris Marion Young, similarly contends that in societies which are increasingly culturally plural there can, nevertheless, be 'a shared public culture which defines the national identity . . . alongside a plurality of private cultures which help define people's identities as members of sectional groups'.[6] He also argues that in most instances and certainly within the UK:

> minority groups do not currently seek to promote their own

identities at the expense of shared national identities: on the contrary, they are often especially eager to affirm their commitment to the nation in order to pre-empt the accusation that their cultural differences must make them disloyal citizens, and for other reasons.

(Miller 2000b: 77; Young 1990)

Miller's approach has clear affinities with Michael Ignatieff's distinction between 'civic' and 'ethnic' nationalism as mutually incompatible ways of envisioning national identity (Ignatieff 1994). This has been recently glossed by Terry McLaughlin as follows:

civic nationalism is democratic in character, envisaging the nation as a community of equal, rights-bearing citizens, patriotically attached to a shared set of political practices and values. In contrast, ethnic nationalism sees civic identity as based on ethnicity rather than citizenship and law. Whilst civic nationalism can be rational, flexible, pluralistic and morally rich, ethnic nationalism is tempted by irrationality, fanaticism and authoritarianism.

(McLaughlin 1997: 27)

None of this, of course, constitutes grounds for complacency. It is much easier to articulate such visions than to achieve them. In the first place, there are still many morally serious conservative thinkers who remain sceptical that so much ethnic, cultural and value diversity can peacefully co-exist within the boundaries of 'one nation'. Second, there are more strident, less reflective voices determined to 'protect' and project an exclusionary nationalism. The response to the publication of the Parekh Report by certain sections of the right-wing press was illustrative. The *Daily Telegraph* fulminated that Home Secretary Jack Straw 'wants to rewrite our history' and quoted Lord Tebbit in support of the view that 'the best way forward is integration rather than separation and cultural ghettos', while Tory MP Gerald Howarth attacked the Report as 'an extraordinary affront to the 94 per cent of the population which is not from ethnic minorities' and opined that 'the native British must stand up for ourselves' (*sic*) (*Daily Telegraph*, 10 October 2000: 1–2).[7] A much more serious challenge to complacency was the recurrence of riots and evidence of open conflict between ethnic groups (as well as between the police and gangs of both white and black youth) in several cities in the north of England in 2001 – most notably in Oldham in May of that year and in Bradford in July. By coincidence, only one week before the Bradford disturbances erupted, Sir Herman Ousely had delivered a devastating report 'Community Pride Not Prejudice' to Bradford City Council, analysing the causes of what the report saw as a history of 'growing divisions among its population'. The eleven-strong panel that produced the Report identified a range of contributory factors that in its view had created 'a unique challenge to race relations' – including: the decline in the city's traditional manufacturing base, white flight and middle-class flight (including Sikhs and Hindus), *de facto* segregation of schools along ethnic and religious lines, the rise of crime, fear on the part of the authorities of confronting the gang and drug culture, ineffectual and unrepresentative 'community leaders', etc. Alongside such openly conflictual manifestations of ethnic tension, it is also self-evidently the case that racism of many kinds continues to disfigure British society at all levels and in all areas of the country – to an extent that has led some to argue that 'the fact that institutional racism persists in liberal societies, including Britain even today, means that the whole basis of democracy and citizenship is constantly undermined' (Osler and Starkey 2000: 4; Macpherson *et al.* 1999). All this, however, arguably constitutes a series of *challenges* to re-imagine and reconstruct national citizenship, rather than grounds for either despair or retreat into anachronistic 'little Englander' attitudes. Indeed, it is possible that in Britain at the beginning of a new century, a more open and inclusive kind of national identification might be one of the most hopeful symbolic foci around which to try to rebuild social solidarity and citizenship.

It is, moreover, by no means implausible to see the European Union as potentially a catalyst rather than as an obstacle to such aspirations – though any assessment of these matters must inevitably be cautious and provisional. Clearly, we can do no more here than offer the barest outline of an argument. For our purposes, what is most important is that, paradoxically, it may be precisely closer integration within the EU which offers the best prospects for building a stronger and more inclusive sense of national identity – or at least the sort of national identity which is founded on a reinforced commitment to social democratic values. As Will Hutton reminded us some time ago:

> It is true as the sceptics argue that European economic and social structures vary, but what unites European states is as striking as their differences. There *is* a broad European model. There *is* a commitment to an inclusive social security system, public health and education systems founded upon progressive taxation of incomes in all European states, including Britain ... The Europeans try to avoid pushing too much risk on to the disadvantaged, to uphold welfare systems, to sustain public goods like education and health, and to run a more productive, higher investing capitalism.
>
> (Hutton 1997: 96, our italics)

The arguments and data we cited in Chapter 1 from Lipset and Marks' (2000) comparative study of the US and Western Europe reinforce this point. The much stronger social democratic traditions of Western European nations may constitute the most important basis for defending social citizenship against the relentless scepticism and even cynicism of the apologists of shareholder capitalism and they do so not only because they embody the values of a distinctive political culture but because that culture is supported by much stronger institutions.

Of course, there is no guarantee that such commitments will be promoted by closer European integration, let alone by enlargement of the EU. Sceptics here point to differing degrees of commitment to welfare among member states, for example, the much weaker traditions of some southern European nations in these respects – as well as the fact that in terms of European citizenship, social rights are separated from political rights and remain largely under national jurisdiction. Many commentators have also noted the powerful pressures towards a 'residualising' of welfare (mainly by replacing entitlements by means-testing) in a context where the 'strategy of "liberalisation" has been justified as the only way of guaranteeing ... economic prosperity in the new global market' (Townsend and Gordon 2000: 4). As these writers have remarked: 'in the 1980s other member states did not believe they should follow that path [of economic liberalism], but some now feel grudgingly obliged, if not to follow suit, to take at least some steps in that direction' (ibid.: 4). They also cite evidence that the last two decades of the twentieth century saw an increase of inequality of both living standards and of poverty in most EU member states. Nevertheless, in a brief but illuminating discussion of the future of European welfare states, Townsend and Gordon point to more optimistic possibilities. They highlight the growing critical reaction against the social polarisation which has followed the widespread deregulation of wages and labour markets, the extension of means-testing, the weakening of progressive taxation, etc., and comment:

> In the UK, there were independent reports such as those of the Channel 4 Commission on Poverty, the Council of Churches on unemployment and the future of work, and the New Economic Foundation on social development, which set out the grounds that a reversal of current trends was feasible and affordable (Townsend 1996). Such reports are common across Europe. There is wide support for modernised social insurance, and more jobs in the public services, and especially for more redistribution and less privatisation in the economy.
>
> (ibid.: 9)

Will Hutton has argued that there has long been considerable latent support in Britain for defending welfare systems and upholding public provision of basic goods like health and education. He suggests that 'these preferences are those which the British would want to make if allowed to express their views free from the hysterical anti-European propaganda – and that they can make them better within the EU than outside it' (1997: 96).

We turn finally to the constitutional and identity aspects of European citizenship and how they might relate to building a stronger but more inclusive sense of national identity within the UK. Here again, there are plenty of indications which point in contradictory directions and we need to stress once more the tentativeness of our arguments. The first point we wish to make connects with our contention in Chapter 1 that in Britain, citizenship is an 'invisible' phenomenon which nevertheless has strong effects. Something similar may also be true of the EU. In his 1998 Reith Lectures, Anthony Giddens highlighted the paradox that 'the EU has become increasingly important in the lives of its citizens at the same time as it is losing popular support' (Giddens 1998: 142), and both aspects of this contention may have even greater force in the aftermath of (partial) monetary union, the establishment of the European Central Bank, the introduction of a common currency, etc. These are major constitutional as well as economic developments and involve a significant surrendering of national sovereignty by a group of member states, with a corresponding strengthening of transnational institutional arrangements. EU membership is also, it should not be forgotten, deeply consequential for the lives of *individual* EU citizens – and in a steadily widening area of their lives (the recent incorporation into UK law of the European Convention on Human Rights is a recent and high profile example). However, as a basis for identity European citizenship is evidently not strong. This may partly be because many of the duties of citizenship are fulfilled at the level of the nation rather than the individual – for example, contributions to the community budget are made via national governments and raised from national taxation (Lewicka and McLaughlin 2001). It is also significant that official definitions of European citizenship now emphasise that it is complementary (if not supplementary) to national citizenship: thus the Treaty of Amsterdam (1997) amended Articles 8 and 8d of the 1992 Maastricht Treaty, stating that 'citizenship of the Union shall complement and not replace national citizenship' (SCAD 1997: 2, cited in ibid.). A further important set of reasons why a sense of European citizenship is weak has to do with the perception of 'democratic deficit' – repeatedly highlighted by both supporters and opponents of closer European integration. Giddens himself concedes that: 'the union has been constructed by political elites; the European Commission is heavily bureaucratic; the European Parliament lacks much influence; and in most countries EU voters take little interest in European elections' (2000a: 160). All this is in addition to the absence of a strong common culture 'territorially concentrated and based on a shared language' (Kymlicka 1995: 76) – while the prospect of enlargement of the EU portends a further cultural 'dilution' (or at least diversification).

However, from the standpoint of building a strengthened but 'modernised' kind of *national* citizenship identity, the current 'halfway house' situation may have certain advantages. Given that there may well be a referendum on replacing sterling with the Euro during New Labour's second term in government, Europe may well turn out to be a key practical as well as symbolic issue which will decisively test how far some British citizens can be detached from narrow and (we would contend) backward-looking forms of national identification. (The contest for the leadership of the British Conservative Party in 2001 illustrated not only how divisive but also how consequential such a decision is likely to be.) In our view, closer European integration need *not* necessarily lead to the centralised, bureaucratic and non-accountable 'federal super-state' so feared by many opponents of closer integration. It could be a development which allows enhanced development of transnational forms of governance in some areas to be combined with significant or even strengthened forms of national and local identification in others – with the possibility of extending democratic forms of accountability and control at both levels. Giddens puts part of the argument as follows:

> The EU is not a super nation state, nor is there any likelihood that it might or could become one. It isn't a form of federalism either. It is difficult to categorise in traditional political terms precisely because it is a novel experiment, an attempt to develop governmental structures different from those that have existed before . . . It might sound odd to offer the EU as an example – the prime example – of democratisation above the level of the nation, since it is so often criticised for its 'democratic deficits' . . . Yet the EU was certainly not constructed against the wishes of the majority of citizens of its member states. Moreover, a range of short- and longer-term measures can be introduced that produce greater democracy as well as more popular legitimacy. Some of the prescriptions for democratising democracy within nations also apply directly to the EU . . . The most problematic issues concern the authority of the European parliament. Undoubtedly there should be a shift in power towards it and away from the Commission.
>
> (Giddens 2000a: 160–1)

This is, clearly, an optimistic scenario but it does point towards what could potentially be achieved in favourable circumstances.

Turning to the possibility that on-going European integration may facilitate a certain sort of strengthening of *national* identities, we would cite the example of devolution within the UK. In the case of Scotland, for example, the European dimension not only had favourable historical resonances going back to the Scottish

Enlightenment and even beyond, it also provided an overarching political and economic framework within which limited devolution could appear both less risky than it might otherwise have seemed as well as being not radically different from the kind of regional autonomy found in, say, the German Länder. This may well have been important in building support for devolution from those Scots who were looking for a middle way between outright independence and subservience to Westminster. For many voters in Scotland, a strengthened 'nested' set of national identities as European/British/Scottish may be a comfortable psychological correlate of these institutional developments. The case of Scotland also illustrates how devolution within the wider European context may lead to a strengthening of aspects of social citizenship. One highly pertinent example for our purposes is the decision of the Scottish Parliament in 2000 to abolish higher education tuition fees – and this is only one example of the stronger commitment to welfare within Scotland. Of course, the question of the effects of Scottish and Welsh devolution on England and on English voters, opens onto a more uncertain terrain. Perhaps as a result of the deep-rooted conflation of 'English' and 'British' in the minds of many people in England, there appears to be very limited support for attempts to emphasise a stronger sense of separate English national identity: the increasingly multicultural make-up of England is also likely to be significant in this respect – and language is not a major issue. In terms of a revival of *social* citizenship, it is likely to be strategically important to hold Britain (or at least mainland Britain) together[8] – albeit as a less tightly bonded entity, not least because the greater affluence of south and south-east England could become a basis for new kinds of self-interested separatist aspirations not dissimilar to those in northern Italy.

The vision of Britain as a 'cosmopolitan nation' (Giddens 1998: 130–2) is still at present just that: a vision. But it may well be one around which support for a new kind of progressive citizenship could be built.

Chapter 3

Citizenship and the restructuring of higher education

3.1 Introduction

To the social democrat living in the 1960s, the growth of higher education from an elite system to one where a third of school leavers take part, could be expected to have an enhancing effect on citizenship. More people going to university might be seen to have the same kinds of social benefits as more people having any type of education. For example, it could be hoped that it would make them better informed about the society in which they live. It might make them more able to deal with the problems facing their society, better able to make a contribution to it, and, perhaps, give them an enhanced feeling for its existence and concern for its fate.

Thirty years on, in official policy documents considering the future of the higher education system, there can still be found references to such benefits for citizenship. In the 1997 Dearing Report, for example, it is acknowledged that:

> higher education continues to have a role in the nation's social, moral and spiritual life; in transmitting citizenship and culture in all its variety; and in enabling personal development for the benefit of individuals and society as a whole.
>
> (NCIHE 1997: Terms of Reference: Annex A)

But for some, these sorts of references to citizenship can now be read very differently. In particular, for those groups of academics and professionals who acquired their higher education qualifications twenty or more years ago, and then used them within the state welfare and educational services, issues of citizenship in relation to higher education now seem very much overshadowed by concerns for national economic competitiveness through individual enterprise. If higher education, in the UK and elsewhere, now has anything to do with citizenship, it is more likely to be seen as being about promoting the active worker-citizen. As one commentator on the changes in higher education in both Australia and the UK expressed it: 'life and citizenship are conflated with work and participation in the economy, particularly in ways which will enhance the competitiveness of the nation's economy in world markets' (Dudley 1999: 90). The question which has to be asked is whether the very ways in which higher education has been extended to a greater percentage of the population, and re-structured to serve the economy, run contrary to earlier democratic and social hopes and aspirations. Do some current developments actually marginalise social understanding, and foster only individual means of dealing with the problems of society, inhibit connection and collective commitment, encourage despair and a general lack of concern for the fate of others? Such critical questioning may lead to one of two conclusions. Either one can see that other identities are being fostered by the extension of higher education, at the expense of that of 'citizen', or a new form of citizenship is being constructed as an alternative to that which the social democratic state tried to promote.

It is as well to admit from the beginning that some academics may have certain problems with these debates. It has been a persistent idea among many who work in higher education and also of certain other professionals, that they are the defenders of citizenship against the market. This has been a particularly strong theme in social science where not only have some shared Durkheim's faith in professional altruism but have also seen the work of academics as involved in the promotion of the right to cultural citizenship (Turner 1993). As a result, and also because of their evolving employment situation, some academics may sound too judgemental about what is happening to their students, their workplace and their society. Others in contrast, perhaps as a reaction, may be too accepting in their descriptions of the changed world in which they imagine young and old now live. We are conscious of the dangers of relying on the reflections about changes within the university sector which derive from employees *of* those institutions. Partly arising from the age profile of academics currently working in UK universities, many of whom were

recruited in the initial period of the expansion of higher education and also educated during a period of student activism, there
is a certain perception that students currently at university are
lacking in social commitment and political consciousness. Indeed,
it would be surprising if UK academics did *not* have grave suspi-
cions about the effects of some of the recent changes in the
funding and management of their places of work, given that
increases in student numbers have not been matched by increases
in funding. One such suspicion is that the financial pressures on
the students themselves are such that they have little time for
politics and activities beyond the combined demands of their
courses and part-time work – leaving them, with their remaining
resources, understandably 'just having a good time'.

Whatever the accuracy of these observations might be, there is
some evidence about the changed nature of student attitudes and
the nature of student activism (e.g. Silver and Silver 1997). But
while it may be accepted that there have been great changes in
both the experience and use of higher education, some of the
reported or presumed reactions appear to be based on highly
selective recollections and contrasts between a social democratic
past and a neo-liberal present and future.

Instead of panic about a presumed lack of social commitment
and political interest, the other main reaction among commentators is to declare that things are just different, and that talk about
higher education and citizenship is now either inappropriate or
needs fundamental revision. Some observations may be used to
suggest this is so. First, it could be claimed that there is no longer
either the 'city' or its national equivalent which has any significance, or with which it is possible to identify. In this view young
people, whether attending university or not, have been born into
a fundamentally different world, in which it would be not only
unrealistic but self-denying to embrace old constructions of 'my
nation', just as it would be out of place to refer to 'my class'.
Certain arguments relating to globalisation may be taken as suggesting this thesis and when applied to higher education, they
might focus upon the way universities have lost their physical
boundaries and exist in a global market (Blight *et al.* 2000).

An extension to this argument is that if the nation has lost any
semblance of coherence, unity or integrity, then so have the
nation's universities. Partly because of 'the universal melting of
identities, dispersal of authorities, and growing fragmentariness of

life which characterise the world in which we live' (Bauman 1997: 21), the universities also become places of difference and fragmentation. For some, indeed, their diversity and incoherence are their strength: 'Only such universities have something of value to offer to the multi-vocal world of uncoordinated needs, self-procreating possibilities and self-multiplying choices' (ibid.: 25).

Observations concerning the changed identity of students may also be included in the view that the world has changed in such a way as to bury the old social democratic dreams. The claim here might be that the importance of being at university, and indeed the definitions of what it is to be a student, have changed in ways which mean that any effects of higher education on a student's less specific social attitudes and sentiments are greatly diminished. National cultural political projects using higher education cannot be effective. The very life of university studentship is now no longer separate, special, insulated or even personally significant. For many it is part-time, enmeshed in domestic life, continuous with earning, caring and just 'being ordinary'.

Where does all this leave any debate surrounding citizenship and higher education? Have the issues been dissolved, if not resolved, by globalisation, difference and diversity? This is difficult to accept. Whether we approve of it or not, many aspects of the restructuring of higher education in the UK have in fact been part of a national political project. Whether it has been initiatives like Enterprise in Higher Education, or the introduction of tuition fees and loans, there have been political attempts to change higher education in a particular direction, and promote a particular kind of citizen. Partly because of this, unease about the changed nature of students' educational experiences and outlook on life persists. Other researchers and commentators seem to find some comfort and significance in what they take to be the fact that students now have very few expectations of the state, a low opinion of politicians, and considerable confidence in their future ability to provide for themselves. For some writers associated with the Adam Smith Institute this is seen as demanding a re-thinking of the whole citizenship education programme. For them, trying to make young people more active citizens 'might simply be inappropriate, given the way in which young people regard their role in the world, and the things they see as important for their own future' (Pirie and Worcester 2000: 9).

The point is, however, that although we may not be justified in seeing all that has occurred in higher education, in the life of students, and the attitudes of young people, as simply the result of a neo-liberal political project, higher education remains part of a set of contested publicly promoted policies, part of differing national projects pursued by political parties. In that minimal sense at least, some aspects of citizenship are still alive and remain part of current political, social and educational debate about the future of higher education. Avoiding the indulgence of an academic retrospect may not necessarily demand nihilistic dismissal, nor the acceptance of a self-styled 'realism'. We might acknowledge that being a citizen is indeed different, and that the functions of universities have changed, but not, perhaps, in the ways that some may fear and others welcome.

Much of the current discussion about both the changes in citizenship and higher education refers, explicitly or implicitly, to two interrelated tendencies: marketisation and globalisation. Where the former refers principally to changes in the nature and structure of higher education institutions, the latter refers to the new contexts in which both citizens and higher education institutions operate. These are so much incorporated in the visions of the future and critiques of the present that, in this chapter, we will look at each in turn, analysing what is understood by these terms and how it is thought such developments change the nature of citizenship and higher education. A number of tensions will be identified which are not always acknowledged in the debate. These derive from the central dilemma that higher education is politically promoted and defended as part of a national project to increase investment in human capital for national competitiveness in what is, nevertheless, widely represented as a globalised economy. At the same time, higher education institutions, and some of their students, are tempted to move beyond national boundaries in a variety of enterprising and entrepreneurial ways.

Marketisation and globalisation are, so often, conceptualised as tendencies at a distance, and are rarely brought down to earth in terms of different effects on different groups of people. This we shall attempt in the following chapters in relation to the ways certain students are currently choosing and using higher education and how this may affect their sense of being a citizen.

3.2 Marketisation of higher education

What has come to be called the marketisation of the public services is widely seen to have certain key effects on the nature of citizenship. This issue is explored by Freedland (2001) where he attempts to demonstrate the way relationships between state or government, citizens, and what he calls the 'intermediate public service providers' are constructed in the process of marketisation. While he acknowledges that the splitting or separation of the political from the administrative has had a long history, connected, for example, with the independence of the civil service (ibid.: 93), the point about the splitting of the providers of a service from the state in the processes of marketisation is that it was aimed at giving the former financial autonomy via competitive funding of providers, where the money follows the user or client of the service. The belief held by those who have sought to introduce market forces into the public services has been that this will promote both efficiency and economy.

There are three relationships which are affected and which could be seen to promote what Freedland calls 'market citizenship' as opposed to public or social citizenship. As far as he is concerned, the most important of the three is the distinctive way in which the relations between the service provider and the state become economised. Here, the government, seeing itself as the purchaser on the part of the citizen, introduces the discourse of financial accountability and audit, which has little directly to do with the actual concerns of the public. For Freedland, although the citizen is formally missing from this relationship between state and service provider, it is here where we can find the most fundamental effects on citizenship. It is here, for example, where performance indicators are imposed which exclude any reference to those affected. The relationship is economised, in the sense that judgements are made before all else on the basis of efficiency and value for money. The other two relationships are those between the service provider and the citizen, and the citizen and the state or government. With marketisation, in the former case the citizen becomes a shopper or customer. In the latter the relation becomes indirect and incidental because the state is at a distance from the market in services. Separate regulatory agencies are constructed by governments to maintain this distance from the public, which is atomised as separate individual consumers.

Through these processes, Freedland sees citizens being marginalised.

There is considerable argument about whether the changes in higher education in the UK can best be seen as effects of the spread of market forces or the extension of central state control or some combination of the two (Middleton 2000). In the case of the institutional development of higher education the situation is quite complex. The separation of purchaser from provider, in the way described by Freedland, did not occur in all colleges and universities as it did in the school system and in some other parts of the welfare state. The Education Reform Act separated the former polytechnics and colleges from their local authorities, and they became independent corporate institutions in 1988, funded, initially by the PCFC. But the so-called 'old' universities already had a separate independent existence, charging subsidised fees paid directly by local authorities.

However, the modelling provided by Freedland remains useful in exploring various recent changes in higher education and also for posing questions about the effects of such changes on citizenship. For many commentators like Rustin (1994), there are sufficient similarities between what has happened in the higher education sector and in other public and welfare services to justify the use of the term marketisation. Crucial in this respect has been the promotion of competition between the now separated 'autonomous' enterprises of higher education. Indeed, the abolition by government of the so-called binary divide between the polytechnics and the original universities, where the former were given university status as a result of the 1992 Further and Higher Education Act, can be seen as part of an assault on a cartel (ibid.: 189). In this move, the 'old' universities were exposed to lower cost producers. In addition, a whole series of innovations concerned with bidding for funds, pressure to recruit extra students on a 'fees-only' basis, and competition for research funding via the Research Assessment Exercise have had clear effects upon the organisation and culture of all institutions of higher education. Academics have been forced to identify markets for their courses, consider different forms of 'delivery' (Henkel 1997: 139) and pursue funds for research from industry and elsewhere. Management styles and techniques from private companies have been introduced into the universities and colleges, with performance-related pay for senior management and the use of input–output models to assess institutional success or failure.

It is clear that many of these changes in the relationship between government and providers have affected the position of academics as employees. Not only were the reforms accompanied by changes to the contracts of those working in higher education (most notably, loss of tenure for many in the 'old' universities), but such changes occurred along with pressures to increase productivity and an intensification of work. This, along with the loss of some powers of democratic decision-making via changes to academic boards and other committees meant that one could say academics lost some of their democratic rights as well as a sense of membership. These changes have convinced some that, with marketisation, 'the wider social purposes of education, which might have formerly been open to democratic – or indeed, academic – control and accountability, are lost' (Ainley 1998: 567).

But what have been the more general effects on citizenship and on students? In Freedland's model it is the use of accounting procedures and the setting of economised targets by the state which are seen as having the most far-reaching effects upon citizenship as a whole, not just on the professionals within the system. Indeed, as Crouch *et al.* suggest, Freedland's analysis sees the 'public employees' interests as allied with those of the public at large' (Crouch 2001: 13). While he does not refer to higher education, his examples both from other parts of the educational system and other public services, do indicate that the use of notions of 'value added' and abstract, de-localised models of service provision that are required by economic accounting procedures, create a system where those who receive the service are quite excluded from any public deliberation of what is worthwhile. To fit into the system of accounting, it is likely that knowledge within higher education itself becomes commodified.

Prioritising the relations between government and providers, as Freedland does, may tend to focus our attention on the effects as seen from the position of the academic employee. It is true that the marketisation of this relationship might also be passed on to students. They may be treated as mass consumers, for example, and there could be a narrowing of concerns for their needs in terms of the kinds of learning and vocational outcomes defined by government. The whole system of accounting also makes it difficult for other interests to be represented in the running of the universities, and may well restrict any public debate about the range of courses which they should offer. However, it is possible to trace some more explicit citizenship effects if we look at the other two relationships Freedland identifies. In the case of higher education, these are those between student and provider, and between the state and student-citizens.

Do contemporary students now see themselves as individual purchasers of a service, with the rights and commitments of a customer? Certainly this was the intention of the Charter for Higher Education, one of the products of the Citizen's Charter programme of the Major government. The overall aim of the Charter project was to encourage more people to actively choose between providers of a service, to exercise their rights as consumers in such a way as to put pressure on bureaucrats, local councillors and others (Faulks 1998: 133). Alongside a number of other initiatives intended to open up public services to competition – including privatisation, contracting out of services and performance-related pay – the aims of the Citizen's Charter were to ensure that the consumer of state services would have the necessary access to relevant information necessary to make informed choices. In the case of the Student's Charter which followed the Citizen's Charter in 1993, it was argued that a broad range of consumers of higher education, including students, employers and the general public, be given all the necessary information to make them informed consumers. It was acknowledged that:

> Customers of universities and colleges also have responsibilities and the Charter reminds you of some of them. But the focus is on the meeting of *your* legitimate needs. If you are not satisfied with the service you receive, the Charter explains what you can do to get it put right.
>
> (DFE 1993: 1–2)

Such government initiatives on their own are unlikely to have much effect on the users. They may rouse opposition and may also focus attention on the particular kind of citizenship which is implied in the notion of the active consumer, where the emphasis is on personal responsibility and individual choosing and not on political participation or holding government to account (Faulks 1998: 138–43). But few read these publications and even fewer are likely to have their relations with the providing bodies, such as universities, changed by them. The indirect effects upon the *employees* may have been greater because, as Tritter (1994) has shown, the charters went hand in hand with the introduction of so-called Total Quality Management initiatives into the public services.

However, there can be no doubt that in their competition for students within a process of marketisation, universities and colleges *have* tried to construct students as customers. This is most obvious in the whole area of recruitment and advertising and the marketing of higher education. Shumar's analysis of the commodification of higher education in the USA (1997) included a chapter on the way competing colleges present themselves to different groups of customers, using the standard marketing methods any other retailer or producer employs. In the case of an institution catering predominantly for students whose parents did not go to college, the emphasis was on affluence and fun. For another, catering more for middle-class students, the images were of graduates getting successful careers, and in the most prestigious institutions the emphasis was on culture and status. No doubt similarly differentiated imagery could be found in the way UK colleges and universities are currently presenting themselves to students.

Indeed, there is a good deal of evidence about the way universities and colleges in Britain are developing the techniques and research to inform their recruitment. For the universities themselves, existing within a competitive, market system, their main concerns are likely to be with recruitment, retention and costs. For them, the important questions are the following. How can we ensure that the range of interests and needs of prospective customers are catered for within the system and at a cost they can afford? Can we improve our systems of delivery in ways that fulfil national requirements articulated by governments and within the budgets which are currently set nationally? Recent British research on entry into higher education has tended to reflect this combination of concerns, and, although not presented as such, some of this work owes much to other consumer research. An example, sponsored by the Committee of Vice-Chancellors and Principals of the Universities of the UK, the Higher Education Funding Council for England, and the University and Colleges Admissions Service (CVCP 1999), declared its aims and orientation thus:

> Increasingly, students are being seen as customers with individual needs and preferences. In this wider and more

competitive higher education market, there is a need to understand better how students make choices about higher education study and what factors influence the choices made.

(ibid.: 1)

At the general level, there is a requirement to understand the different groups of consumers and their expectations, conceptualised in the report as 'Diversity and Market Segmentation'. At the more specific level, there is a need to know how prospective students-as-customers approach the business of choosing higher education, what they decide, when, how and why.

Once enrolled, there are a number of changes in the experience of being a student which could be seen as part of the marketisation of higher education and thus as having the effect of extending the consumer–provider relationship. Take, for example, the way new student accommodation is now provided and financed. Old universities provided accommodation in halls of residence, many of which were originally funded by university benefactors. A number of other higher education institutions including teacher training colleges, also provided such accommodation, which was managed as part of the overall academic-pastoral mission, influenced by notions of *in loco parentis*. For most institutions, the situation now is quite different. Where accommodation linked to the college or university is available, it is managed and financed in ways similar to other commercial property, priced at levels to cover both running costs and capital construction (Blakey 1994).

The ways in which many university courses are now organised and 'delivered' may also be seen to develop the identity of student-consumer. Various forms of credit transfer and modularisation could appear to encourage the orientation to higher education as one in which the individual can 'shop around' for components of a degree, with only limited involvement with any one institutional provider. These developments in curricular construction and delivery can also be seen to drive out the possibilities for critical and reflexive thought, particularly when tied in to the 'sale' of competencies to students for use in subsequent employment. Winter develops this point as follows:

> university courses are increasingly being recast into integrated systems of 'modular' units, allowing students to construct

their own 'customised' courses by selecting their own combination of modules. This means that higher education staff no longer have responsibility for designing a sequence of learning experiences which might profoundly affect student identities; instead they merely make available a circumscribed fragment of expertise within a computerised system of options.

(1999: 190)

However, relating what are essentially cultural critiques of such developments – the marketisation of higher education, the commodification of culture, and loss of collegiality – to issues of citizenship is highly problematic. There are a number of reasons why it is necessary to be cautious about seeing these kinds of changes in higher education as having any direct effects on relations between providers and students and in turn, producing either a new form of citizenship or somehow making social democratic citizenship impossible.

First, as with the other developments outlined above, it is necessary to distinguish between the effects on academics, on managers and on different groups of students. In one sense, marketisation affects both academic and student because so many of the changes which have claimed to be about constructing and empowering the consumer have also been concerned with managing and controlling the employee. For example, developing customer-oriented cultures in colleges and universities has been accompanied by the introduction of Human Resource Management policies with destructive effects on professional identities and working relationships in some institutions (Esland *et al.* 1999). Winter himself was conscious of the dangers of criticising the commodification of higher education only from the point of view of the academic:

> It is not helpful to react with nostalgia, contrasting the malign logic of the market (mediated through the power of a profit-oriented management) with a supposed 'golden age' when the craft of the academic was simply the direct expression of moral value, educational need and the search for truth.
>
> (ibid.: 194)

Yet even if one has no wish to return to such a golden age of

'donnish dominion' (Halsey, 1992), as far as citizenship is concerned, one has to accept that some aspects of improving rights of
access to higher education for a variety of different age and social
groups by providing flexibility of study, *are* likely to have problematic effects on the forms of contract of employment and
conditions of service of at least a significant proportion of academics.

Another reason why it is so difficult to distinguish and identify
the effects of marketisation on students is that the student has not
been legally re-constituted as a consumer. There does exist a contract between student and university which is subject to the same
regulations as other contracts, and students are increasingly
turning to the courts to deal with problems (Evans and Gill 2001)
but the legal identity of 'university' has remained unclear. The
Citizen's Charter and the Student's Charter had no legal force
and bestowed no new legal rights (Tritter 1994). As Cawkwell and
Pilkington (1994) argued, universities have accumulated a whole
set of legal and cultural powers over the years which sustain what
these writers term a 'quasi-judicial power over students' concerning ethics, discipline and community life (ibid.: 82). In such ways,
some of the remnants of collegiality remain.

But perhaps the strongest point which critics make concerning
the links between marketisation of public services and citizenship
is that such developments *drive out* or make impossible democratic
procedures and inclinations. At the national level it is claimed
that the state and government protects itself from criticism and
responsibility by setting up quangos and other intermediate
bodies to oversee the internal markets. In Freedland's terms, the
relationship between student-citizen and the state becomes marginalised. At the local level, any collective democratic decision-
making is also undermined. In reaction to the attempts to
develop an internal market in schooling, for example, such critics
have used Hirschmann's (1970) distinction between 'voice' and
'exit' to highlight what they see as a political process. Ranson, for
example, described the situation as follows:

> the administered market in education seeks to fetter local
> elected representatives and professionals, as the bearers of
> the old order, and emancipate the middle class as the bearers
> of the new ... As power shifts and relationships alter, the old
> polity become unrecognisable and a distinctively different

political order emerges. 'Exit' replaces 'voice' as the mechanism by which a society takes allocative decisions.

(1996: 220–1)

While it may be true that the particular combination of managerialism for the employees and limited consumerism for the students makes sustaining certain democratic procedures difficult, the construction of students as individualised consumers has, nevertheless, not been completed – and, as we shall argue later, it *could* not be completed. What has in effect emerged, on many campuses and nationally, is a combination of consumerism and citizenship, exemplified most clearly perhaps in the evolving activities of students unions. In 1992 the National Union of Students produced its own Student's Charter declaring certain rights for all students (NUS 1992) and in subsequent years, institutional charters have been negotiated which dealt with the academic entitlements of all students, and their democratic rights of participation (Silver and Silver 1997: 167). While such charters often deal with students as a group, some student unions have also been involved in the development of Learning Agreements, which are intended to give students clear statements of what they can expect as individuals (Opacic 1994). True there is a predicament for student unions in the extent to which they become campaigners on behalf of consumers and some student activists have reservations about the trends in student political awareness; moreover, some student union presidents interviewed in the Silvers' study saw their fellow students as 'Thatcher's children' focused only on their own individual futures (Silver and Silver 1997: 122–3). Notwithstanding various attempts to change their nature, student unions do remain public, democratic forums in which inequalities, injustices, etc. can be discussed, along with complaints about 'mis-selling', contract failure and day-to-day problems with accommodation and other facilities. This combination of issues has become most explicit in the case of recent national campaigns concerned with student tuition fees and loans, and it is to this most important aspect of marketisation that we must now turn.

Of all the changes to higher education in the UK, the gradual but definite privatisation of the funding must be the area which could be expected to have the most direct effect on students and their sense of citizenship. Indeed, when student loans were first discussed, changing students' attitudes was presented as one of the key aims of the proposed reforms: 'We wish to encourage self-reliance and individual responsibility among students' declared the then Secretary of State for Education and Science, John MacGregor (Hansard 1989: 158). He went on to reject a graduate tax because it would 'singularly lack that benefit of culture and attitude which a loans scheme has, of encouraging students to see their higher education as an investment that they are making in themselves for themselves' (ibid.: 158, 381). It was also thought that because they would be investing some of their own money, students would be more inclined to insist that they obtain value for it in their courses. The hope was that such a change would make higher education institutions more responsive to consumer demands, and higher education institutions would need to demonstrate that their courses produced career benefits, and to market them accordingly (Howarth 1991).

In July 1997 the National Committee of Inquiry into Higher Education reported its findings, putting together further arguments why students should contribute to their own higher education (NCIHE 1997). A key argument was that not only did students personally benefit from obtaining a degree by subsequently earning more money, but these benefits were unevenly distributed between economic groups because of uneven recruitment into higher education from the different social classes. The Labour Government accepted the main principles, and subsequently scrapped means-tested grants altogether and introduced a system of means-tested tuition fees and loans. There are many ways in which the replacement of grants by loans and fees is different from some other internal and quasi-market initiatives in the public services. Compared to marketisation in the school system, for example, this does seem to be a move towards truly private markets. While one of the effects of local financial management in schools was to encourage an increase in money-raising activities by parents, this was not part of the system of funding as such. In fact, the current system of finance of UK higher education is difficult to characterise. Middleton describes it as follows:

> It can be argued that higher education has developed as a quasi market with demand based on a hybrid arrangement: some funding depending on a single state purchaser, the rest on a voucher scheme with choice exercised by the direct consumers.
>
> (2000: 545)

He calls it a voucher system because loans are guaranteed and not charged at commercial rates of interest, however, that is probably not how the borrowers see it! Again, we must beware of viewing loans from the perspective of academic employees. Paying tuition fees, and borrowing money for one's higher education may well have quite different personal effects from other recent reforms in higher education. Because it is not about 'enclosed' purchasing within an internal market, its effects may not be so problematic for the day-to-day work of academics and their relations with the state. Indeed, to the extent that the extra money from tuition fees may come into the system, then their own income and security may increase. But as far as citizenship and the student are concerned, there is a clear move from previously existing citizenship rights in higher education towards market provision. Even though previous grants were means-tested, they were an *entitlement*, and there was no payment of tuition fees, regardless of personal or parental income.

Within this new system students do appear to become individual purchasers of a service, using their own money, and increasingly carrying the risks in a contract with the provider, and the Student Loan Company. Margison (1997) uses some aspects of Foucauldian theory to explore the effects on the subjectivities of the students themselves of similar developments in Australia. For him, the loan system for higher education is just part of the neo-liberal project to 'ground the norms of an enterprise economy in all the theatres of social life' (ibid.: 119). Education becomes 'a market in self-investment,' and the student becomes an 'investor in the self; ... the student-citizen imagined in an earlier era of policy is replaced by a competitive economic subject motivated by individual utility' (ibid.: 122). His point is that in a situation where higher education is free, or costs to the individual are low, there is limited scope for students to calculate as investors in terms of returns, but this can be changed when charges accrue directly to the individuals. They are, in a sense, burdened by greater costs yet 'empowered' as investors in the self. Margison does admit in his conclusion that there is limited evidence of shifts in the subjectivities of higher education students, and much is anecdotal, as we note above. Yet his paper is built upon a set of statements about the effects of loan systems for higher education which are based upon direct contrasts between the 'student-citizens' of the past, with their universal rights to education, and the new competitive economic subjects managing themselves and choosing their career options. True, the latter are at times referred to as 'imagined' (ibid.: 122), but one does need, at some point, to question the relations between the constructions of neo-liberal political rhetoric and the experiences and self-understandings of those living through the changes.

In the following chapters we shall attempt to provide some limited empirical observations on these matters, but there are two general points which need to be made with regard both to the citizenship effects of marketisation of higher education in general, and the use of fees and loans in particular. These call into question any straightforward re-definition of citizenship as implied in both neo-liberal rhetoric and some of the reactions to it.

First, we know little about what students actually understand about the general financing of their higher education within the new system. Although loans and fees have been introduced, it is the *state* which remains the major source of funding for what is still in many respects a national system. Indeed, for writers like Tooley (1997) this may be regarded as a matter of regret, as he thinks it encourages the inflation of qualifications and under-mines culture because of the 'cosy relationship academics have with the state' (ibid.: 15). From the perspective of student-citizens, however, a key issue is the extent to which they still see themselves in receipt of public funds derived from taxation. Official publications addressing prospective students and inform-ing them of their financial position suggest that although they may have to pay over £1,000 per annum tuition fees, this remains a bargain as the real cost is £4,000, with the difference made up by the state (DFEE 1999b; Ahier 2000). However, if students have no accurate knowledge about the balance between private and public funding, it is possible that what is a very partial privatisa-tion may have an unintended long-term 'educational' effect. Recent graduates may be convinced that they did indeed pay for their own higher education, and therefore feel that those who come after them should do likewise. Much would depend upon the political representation of alternatives, and the extent to which access to higher education is advanced as a right.

When one looks at the actual sources of finance used by stu-dents during their higher education it is clear that for certain groups, being a student continues to mean being a dependant. What has happened is that dependence upon the state has been replaced, at least in part, by dependence upon *family*, and this may be of increasing significance (Winn and Stevenson 1997; Walters and Baldwin 1998; Callender and Kemp 2000). Thus, the system of loans and fees increases the private share of the costs, but not necessarily to the *individual* consumer. For many students who are entering university from school, loans and fees do not turn them into *individualised*, independent consumers of higher education as envisaged by the initial promoters of loans. They remain, at best, semi-dependent users of a state service. Their connections with their families are significant, both because the level of fees and loans available depends upon their parents' disposable income, and also because many parents are intimately involved in both the choosing and financing of higher education (see Ahier 2001). Students who have left home and school for some considerable period may be more likely to act or see themselves as independent, individual calculating investors in self. However, even they are likely to be embedded in domestic, private or communal forms of participation which inform and partly determine their higher education experiences and decisions.

This brings us to a key issue in any consideration of the citizenship effects of a change in public policy. The central point is that citizen and customer are artificial constructs. They refer to different forms of social participation, not to the lives as lived by people, or actual institutional outcomes. Not only that, but, as Crouch (2001) points out, within many arguments over citizenship and markets, the third form of participation, that of community is often excluded. In this paper Crouch outlines the three forms of social participation as follows. 'Customership' refers to the purchase of goods in a free market. In 'citizenship' goods are allocated as of right. In 'community' custom and affect determine the allocation of goods, as in families, where universal values do not apply and there are not processes of appeal to rights claims. In both 'community' and 'citizenship', the financing is separated from acquisition. One form of participation does not necessarily exclude, replace or contradict the other. Instead one may find numerous examples of their co-existence, because members of communities are also embedded in the formal relations of citizenship and markets. Crouch refers to the way people claim their rights to a state pension, for example, so that they may take part in the markets in goods and services. In the case of higher education the old grant system enabled students to be mobile customers of a wide range of universities by their use of public funds. This does not mean that some of the recent attempts to construct markets in both higher education and schools are without problems. Crouch identifies three difficulties which can arise from what he calls the 'new ascendancy of the customer principle over that of the citizen' (ibid.: 113). These are distortion, degradation and residualisation. However, a consideration of students' three forms of social participation does enable us to look at a range of effects of recent marketisation of post-school education. Crouch's own work, for example, while not concerned with higher education, shows how some changes in school policies such as the development of local management of schools actually produced an expansion of a certain kind of active citizenship, community and customership (ibid.: 120).[1]

In summary, the effects of marketisation, in the sense of changes to the ways higher education institutions relate to one another, to the state, to their students and employees, are diverse and complex. As far as the students are concerned, this is likely to depend upon their social and economic location. The reason for this is that the student-citizens themselves are so differently located with regard to both their access to the means to participate as customers and as members of communities and families.

3.3 Higher education and globalisation

We must now turn to the concept of globalisation to understand the nature of the support currently given by the UK government to the growth in numbers receiving higher education, but in a form which encourages marketisation and the movement of costs to individuals. For our purposes, three uses of the term globalisation need to be distinguished. First, in some of the more critical sociological literature on higher education, globalisation is used chiefly to refer to the spread of the ideology and practices of marketisation across the world's universities. In a book entitled *Universities and Globalization: Critical Perspectives* by Currie and Newson (1998), it is this approach which predominates. The book claims to throw light on 'how a globalising political economy affects the way universities are governed and how the daily lives of academics have been affected by globalisation practices' (ibid.: 1). The belief is that academics everywhere are suffering from the shift towards 'business values' (ibid.: 2) and the cult of managerialism and accountability. While we accept that there is a case for claiming that public services in a number of countries may indeed show a certain convergence in this respect, and that a whole group of workers employed by the state and including university lecturers are experiencing such changes, there is another often closely associated use of the term which is more open to question and debate. In particular, references to the globalised economy, often used to *justify* the marketisation of higher education in one country, remain open to debate. Third, there is the general characterisation of globalisation as the compression of time and space, and the increase in the quantity and velocity of the flows of information, people, capital and goods. True, such observations are often attached to further claims about the fundamentally new world of late or postmodernity in which we all supposedly now live, but the two kinds of changes can, in principle be distinguished from each other.

In examining these issues in more detail, we shall look first at the level of UK national political-educational discourse. Here the concept of globalisation is used, in the second of the senses we have distinguished, to indicate the supposed new economic environment. This globalised economy – so it is claimed – explains why we need more of the population educated to a higher level, why we cannot use other means to improve both our individual fortunes and those of the nation, and why, increasingly, we have to pay for higher education as private individuals investing in ourselves. Second, we shall then consider developments within higher education to discuss the extent to which universities themselves are subject to global changes and are becoming global institutions. Our analysis will suggest the contradictory nature of the global rhetoric, and its role in attempts to change the nature of citizenship.

3.3.1 Globalisation and current political-educational rhetoric

Within a variety of government texts certain shifts in the global economy are seen as significant as far as the place of higher education in national well-being is concerned. Official characterisations of globalisation can be gleaned from a number of these publications, speeches of ministers and other sources, which indicate the changes, outline the threats, and establish education as the main means to deal with both the problems and the opportunities. Such uses of 'globalisation' and its cognates leach into almost every government education policy document, setting the scene, describing the environment in which the policy has meaning, etc. Certain features of the global context are repeatedly identified: rapidity of change in types of employment arising from growth in the knowledge-based economy, high mobility of capital, and increasing national competition.

Significantly and symptomatically, no alternative is conceived, except that we, as a nation, might fail to keep up, and this is made more difficult by other nations using the same, educational means to get ahead. Fears are increased by citing international comparisons of educational achievement. In *The Learning Age: A Renaissance for a New Britain* (DFEE 1998) for example, in a section called 'The scale of the challenge', it is claimed that 'The country's current learning "scoreboard" shows strengths and weaknesses', and included are comparisons of percentages of populations of different countries with certain levels of qualifications. Few ends are considered for the nation and its education system, other than meeting the challenge and adapting. Take, for example, the report from the National Advisory Committee on Creative and Cultural Education significantly entitled *All Our Futures* (DFEE 1999c). The scene is set by the following: 'Countries throughout the world are re-organising their educational systems. Like us, they are engulfed in rapid economic and social change' (ibid.: 18). It notes that there are:

> radical transformations world-wide in both the nature and the patterns of work ... Whereas the dominant global companies used to be concerned with industry and manufacturing, the key corporations are now in the fields of communications, information, entertainment, science and technology.
>
> (ibid.: 18–19)

Similarly, in *The Learning Age* (DFEE 1998), it is claimed that: 'We are in a new age – the age of information and of global competition. Familiar certainties and old ways of doing things are disappearing. We have no choice but to prepare for this new age' (ibid.: 9). Competition within what is now seen as an open global system is fierce because trans-national companies now use workers from anywhere in the world on the basis of available skills ... these economic shifts are operating independently of national boundaries. Young people need to have high level skills for this complex new world of global markets and competition.

(ibid.: 20)

If such a view of globalising tendencies provides the context in which anxiety about national education in general is generated, it has given a particular urgency to the place of *higher* education and its marketisation. In the Dearing Report (NCIHE 1997), following a standard representation of economic integration, two of the most important implications for higher education are expressed as follows:

High quality, relevant higher education provision will be a key factor in attracting and anchoring the operations of global corporations because of the research capability of its institutions, and the skills and knowledge it can develop in the local workforce.

Higher education itself will become more strongly an international service, with students and employers choosing, on a global basis, the programmes they require, delivered in ways and at times that suit them, making use of new communications and information technologies.

(ibid.: para. 4.14)

Universities are seen to trade in the crucial element in globalised production (knowledge) and in the light of this, British higher education institutions could be seen to have some competitive advantage. They teach in the global language, English, now have corporate freedoms to franchise and export (see above), and they have a global reputation (DFEE 1998: 10). The universities themselves are therefore encouraged to enter the global marketplace on their own account. Prime Minister Tony Blair, in his Romanes lecture at Oxford in 1999, argued that 'universities, particularly the world leaders, compete in an increasingly international market for research, staff and students', adding that less than a third of Oxford's income now comes from Government's Higher Education Funding Council:

In the knowledge economy, entrepreneurial universities will be as important as entrepreneurial businesses, the one fostering the other ... We look to the universities not only as the guardians of traditions of humane learning, but also as one of our key global industries of the future.

(Blair 2000)

A few months later, the then Education and Employment Secretary, David Blunkett, at a lecture at the University of Greenwich, announced the e-universities consortium initiative and Two Year Foundation Degrees. In this lecture he linked up globalisation and marketisation in the following way: 'The arrival of the knowledge economy has intensified the competitive pressures on higher education institutions. Learning has become big business. So a new national initiative is needed to maximise Britain's chances of success in this global environment' (Blunkett 2000). To play their part in national survival, higher education institutions must not only form global alliances but also link more closely with national and local business. Blunkett reiterated the notion of globalisation as that to which we adapt, arguing that this should be accomplished via local openness to business:

Universities need to adapt rapidly to the top-down influences of globalisation and the new technologies, as well as the bottom-up imperatives of serving the local labour market, innovating with local companies, and providing professional development courses that stimulate economic and intellectual growth.

(ibid.)

If the universities do not adapt, then they face the same threat as any business: 'The "do nothing" universities will not survive – and it will not be the job of government to bail them out' (ibid.). Here it is significant that universities do have a right to public funds, but only so far as they fulfil a national role in relation to demands of a global system.

3.3.2 Globalisation of higher education and citizenship

As far as the citizen is concerned, there is something potentially odd about these uses of the concept of gobalisation to instil action and change in a nation's universities and schools. The reason is that to the extent to which they make themselves global, these educational institutions would behave just like any other global enterprise, expecting and owing no national allegiances. Educational institutions, perceived as one of the few means by which government can influence the nation's place in globalised competition, could ironically become just another part of the problem. Global universities would presumably recruit staff and students internationally, sell their qualifications and intellectual property anywhere in the world, reinvest and disinvest across national boundaries, compete with other global institutions for research funds and students, and so on. Different kinds of qualifications could be produced in different parts of the world, and low-cost servicing of students could be carried out in locations where the appropriate labour costs prevailed. Virtual universities could be constructed and maintained by global corporations.

It may, indeed, be tempting to see some current developments in the institutions, their staff, and their students, as stages in such a globalisation of higher education. And no doubt it appeals to many presidents, rectors, vice-chancellors and others who attend meetings of the League of World Universities to claim that theirs are, indeed, global universities, existing in 'intellectual free trade zones' for the transfer of knowledge, faculty and students (www.nyu.edu/rectors/2001abstract.html). The institutions of higher education do appear to transcend national boundaries. The so-called mega-universities involved in distance leaning, like the Open University in the UK, may represent the trend most explicitly (Campion and Freeman 1998), but many others now also enter global networks, develop joint degree programmes, and so on. The new managers of higher education institutions are for ever outward-looking, searching opportunities, and including international activities in their institutional missions. There is another sense, too, in which universities are connected into global processes. Many are increasing their involvement with research and development for transnational or multinational corporations (Slaughter 1998).

Their ordinary academic staff, too, are increasingly pressured to be international via such policies in the UK as the Research and Assessment Exercise: 'The wandering scholar of the Middle Ages may have been replaced by the jet-setting conference-hopper, who in turn may be in the process of being superseded by the information technology revolution with its potential for teleconferencing' (Scott, 1998: 112).

Unions representing university teachers are not unaware of the problems which now arise from what is represented as the involvement of universities in the globalisation of trade and the development of higher education as a commodity in the global market. In the UK, ethical guidance has been issued to union members who find themselves involved in recruiting overseas students, franchising courses overseas, and carrying out international research (AUT and DEA 1999).

As for the students, the expansion in numbers going to universities has been seen as a global phenomenon and with this growth has come increased mobility. More students now study away from their home country and for some there are the possibilities of studying for a single qualification in more than one country, via the accumulation of course credits. There is much evidence of what the OECD has called the internationalising of higher education, both in terms of flows of students and curriculum developments (OECD 1996). Moves are also being made, since the signing of the Bologna Declaration by twenty-nine European countries, to standardise higher education qualifications internationally to make such global qualifications easier to obtain. Even if their study is concentrated in their own country, many students include years away, either during or before their course. For convinced globalists the future can be described as follows:

> Within fifty years and certainly by the end of the first century of the new millennium, the total numbers experiencing higher education will have risen world-wide. The attraction to individuals is that successful higher education will become the principal passport to global citizenship, bestowing upon individuals the capacity to live, work, travel, communicate and participate in local and global affairs.
>
> (Robertson 2000)

These visions of a globalised economy in general, and also of the ways universities, academics and students are somehow apparently freeing themselves from the nation–state and entering a global system, clearly pose considerable problems for any concept of nation-based citizenship. One implication is that national governments can do little to protect their citizens from the flows of labour, capital and currencies in global markets by intervening in the decisions of corporations or investors. At best, they can enable individual citizens to insert themselves *into* these markets by removing any restrictions on their investment, whether in human or financial capital. However, there are a number of criticisms and reservations about both the nature and the implications of globalisation, which have some bearing on the issues we discuss in this book. It is possible to accept that certain things have changed; increases in speed and density of communications, mobility of people and capital, interdependence of economic activities and of environmental well-being, yet still reject the implication that the place of the nation–state, national politics and national citizenship is radically diminished.

First it is important to recognise that, at least in part, the global economy is a construction of nation–states. After all, it was certain governments which were party to actively constructing the global system since the 1970s by their legislative programmes of deregulation, and certain of these governments continue to promote further deregulation internationally. It is therefore possible to see globalisation as a political project itself, associated with the New Right, and not something that has just inevitably occurred as part of the flowering of late modernity, or, indeed, as a result of certain immanent tendencies of late capitalism. As Scott expresses it, 'neo-liberalism and deregulation are intertwined' (1997: 11). He argues that states are key in both the extension of markets and their regulation to protect communities, and that no final 'victory' is possible, as deregulation requires re-regulation in turn.

One sign that national boundaries remain significant is the way different nations have actually reacted to the 'mobilities' taken as characterising globalisation. Not only are there great differences in the extent to which national economies are open or exposed to international flows, national governments also place different emphasis on the claimed benefits. Contrary to the idea represented in political-educational rhetoric above, where the urgency is to keep up with other internationalising economies, it may be that the UK is, in a sense, 'over-internationalised'. Recent work by Hirst and Thompson shows that, in comparison with other industrial countries in the G7 group, the UK is heavily dependent upon overseas trade, its manufacturing sector is increasingly dominated by firms owned elsewhere, and UK pension funds and banks send larger amounts of domestic capital abroad than do those in many other countries (Hirst and Thompson 2000). They conclude that: 'The future of UK citizens' welfare benefits, and their living standards generally, are more fully "mortgaged" to the vagaries of the international economy than are those in the other large advanced economies' (ibid.: 348).

As far as the vision of the globalisation of higher education is concerned, then, it should not be forgotten that most universities have been created by nation–states, and are now more dependent than ever on state support – principally from taxation (Scott 1998). Along with this, they are subject to increased controls and direction, as noted above, and one of the directions promoted by many governments is openness to *local* industry, and sensitivity to *local* labour markets.

Furthermore, even commentators like Slaughter (1998) who describes what she calls the globalisation of academic capitalism, cannot ignore the continuing divergences between national higher education systems. From the point of view of students, this is particularly noticeable in relation to amounts and types of support for study (see NCIHE 1997: Appendix 5). The actual flows of students and academics, while not now reflecting the old ties of empire, do still largely follow the fortunes of both specific nations and of social groups within them. Many students from countries in the Asian-Pacific region, such as Malaysia, Hong Kong and Singapore now attend universities in the UK and USA. One of the reasons is that those countries have developed sectors of the middle class with surpluses to spend on higher education, but have not always been seen to have the appropriate higher education institutions themselves (Scott 1998: 117).

This fact points to a crucial issue for citizenship. It is that higher education institutions are involved in the reproduction of economic *groups* which originate and have their basis within national economies. In the UK the differentiated national system of higher education has been and continues to be used to secure or improve class position with different classes and fractions of classes employing different strategies (Goldthorpe 1996; Pugsley 1998; Reay 1998; Ball *et al.* 2002). With the privatisation of funding via loans and fees, the financial assets of the students' families are likely to have *increasing* effects upon post-school choices (Ahier 2000). It is true that a small, but increasing number of UK students will obtain their university qualifications abroad, mostly in the USA (Kelly 2001). A larger group will use their higher education qualifications to enter international labour markets and international companies based in a number of global cities. For these, the world may indeed seem a small place, and its national boundaries a mere inconvenience. But for most other students, higher education qualifications are being used to secure or improve their employment chances locally or, at best, nationally. Indeed, they rely upon the state to legally enforce exclusion of those without qualifications, from certain areas of work, and many continue to rely upon employment by the state itself to cash in their investment in higher education.

For writers like Reich (1991) who accept the economic globalisation thesis, there is an awareness that the process may have problematic social effects, as some are left behind. He pointed to the possibility that some who can use their qualifications in a world market may be tempted to 'slip the bonds of national allegiance, and by so doing disengage themselves from their less favoured fellows' (ibid.: 3). Critics of the globalisation thesis like Hirst and Thompson (1996), are less impressed by the claims about population mobility. Indeed, they suggest that, for most people, this has become more *restricted*:

> apart from a 'club class' of internationally mobile, highly skilled professionals, and the desperate poor migrants and refugees who endure almost any hardship to leave intolerable conditions, the bulk of the world's population now cannot easily move. Workers in advanced countries have no 'frontier' societies like Australia or Argentina to migrate to as they did ... In the absence of labour mobility states will retain powers over their peoples: they define who is and who is not a citizen, who may and may not receive welfare. In this respect, despite the rhetoric of globalisation, the bulk of the world's population live in closed worlds.
>
> (ibid.: 181)

The role of universities and their degree-conferring capacity is interesting here. They do enable some of their students to enter an international labour market, and they do recruit some international academics to teach them. Indeed, some universities in the UK are currently considering charging differential fees partly because they see themselves competing in international markets for academic staff, students and research funds. If successful, it is difficult to see either the staff or the students of those institutions developing any strong sense of national collective fate. But for most students, in the present and foreseeable future, 'slipping the bonds of national allegiance' is not possible. 'Becoming a graduate', in a society where one-third of the working population will be so qualified, will remain part of the construction of national membership and adulthood, but only rarely the means of moving out.

What effects all this might have on their sense of national citizenship it is difficult to tell. It may be too easy to assume that the combination of globalisation rhetoric and the marketisation of universities in itself just constructs new citizens. Many commentators have certainly pointed to the way globalisation is used to promote only one future, and how globalisation and its assumed impact on education is 'ideologically packaged' (Carnoy 2000). Such rhetoric is used to justify only a particular set of policies, the apparently practical common-sense politics of fitting the nation to global reality, and modernising the economy to fit the new situation. There is, in such visions, no place for citizens to stand back and protect themselves collectively from the demands of global change, for these are seen as universal and external economic trends. Holding back 'global tendencies' is not an option. Within that same political rhetoric there are a number of things which citizens can do, as individuals and members of families – and, in the interests of equality of opportunity, government offers some assistance. First and foremost they can help themselves by improving their skills and investing in their human capital – and governments can help them with loans. After that, again with government encouragement, they can save, insure, take out stakeholder pensions and the like. Individuals can even invest in global equities via revised Personal Equity Plan regulations as well as Individual Savings Accounts.

However, because so much emphasis is placed upon change and uncertainty, and the need to be flexible, any secure collective settlement is denied. Indeed, the main way in which the state itself appears to deal with such flux is to *mirror the open competitiveness of the global market itself.* Thus the institutions of higher education have to become competitive internally and externally, and, in turn, their students need to become more active choosers, and more competitively entrepreneurial. It might be assumed that a new kind of citizen is being constructed: an active, self-improving and competitive subject, whose actions benefit the society as a whole because they reflect the ways of the world. However, this remains an assumption, and one needs to investigate whether the rhetoric and institutional changes are being successful in constructing such 'post social democratic' citizens.

There are at least two areas in which other possibilities may arise. First, as far as graduates are concerned, then a perception of self-interest may lead to the re-assertion of old expectations of the state in the field of employment. For example, in the case of young people who take out loans to gain a degree, we do not know whether globalisation rhetoric merely increases their sense of risk via exposure to graduate competition from elsewhere, or whether getting a degree leads them to have a sense of *entitlement* within the nation. It is not clear if students and graduates are happy to join the international army of graduate-workers. It may be that they expect the state to in some way 'manage' a situation in which there is a potential 'congestion' of graduates, as it has previously done, for example via increases in state employment (Jordan 1998). Current research on the parents of undergraduates certainly suggests that they are aware of credential inflation and believe the state has obligations to those it has persuaded into higher education (Ahier 2001).

The second area in which assumptions may be questioned concerns levels of taxation. Here it has been believed that a globalised economy, where capital, executives and top professionals are so mobile, makes it impossible to raise corporate or personal taxes above levels of competing nations. Not only that but it is assumed that the middle classes as a whole are particularly tax-resistant. These two claims are also open to question and qualification (Chen 1999). A recent survey suggests that while there is a dislike of tax, people are prepared to pay more if there was some hope that services would improve (Commission on Taxation and Citizenship 2000). It might be thought that future graduates are among those least likely to support increases in direct taxation, as they are more likely to find themselves paying back individual loans, contributing to individual pensions, and in jobs which enable them to have private health insurance. Marketisation and globalisation might combine to convince many that services are best when bought with one's own money, and the state can no longer buck the global trends. But again, this orientation is likely to depend upon the capacity of the national economy to provide high levels of well-paid graduate employment. Graduate-citizens would also have to accept that those currently not in receipt of privately funded provision, including perhaps members of their own families, deserve to receive the residual returns of a diminished welfare state. At the same time, they would have to believe that their own qualifications will somehow protect them from having to depend upon the state in the future.

Part II

Graduate citizens?

Evidence and interpretation

Introduction

Chapter 3 has indicated that although there is now an abundance of evidence concerning the recent restructuring of higher education in Britain, there is little consensus about the significance or likely effects of these changes, especially as far as the 'clients' of HE institutions are concerned. We have also noted a tendency in some research on higher education for theorisation to run ahead of evidence – particularly evidence about the *subjectivities* of those students who are already within higher education or are contemplating entering it (for example, Margison 1997). Although these deficiencies are to some extent now being remedied in the case of research which explores the subjective rationalities of young people *applying* to higher education (Ahier 2001; Ball *et al.* 2002), there is still remarkably little evidence about students already 'in the system'.

Our discussion in Part II of this book is intended to make a small contribution to increasing the stock of knowledge and understanding in this neglected area. We interviewed a group of students who were all final year undergraduates at two universities – the University of Cambridge and the Cambridge campus of Anglia Polytechnic University (APU). Because of our interest in citizenship issues, we selected students who were taking courses which contained either a strong Arts or Social Science element and/or who were following vocational or prevocational courses preparing them for entering such public service occupations as teaching, or in some cases, youth work or social work. The basic rationale for this focus was that if *any* current higher education students were going to display interest in and involvement in citizenship issues (especially commitments to *social* citizenship), they might be expected to be found among those taking courses of this kind. In saying this, we are not, of course, claiming that our small sample was either large enough or sufficiently representative to constitute a 'critical case'. Nor were we setting out to test a clearly formulated set of hypotheses. What we hoped to do was more modest. By talking with such students about their perceptions of what being a graduate meant to them, their experience of recent developments like student loans and tuition fees, their career aspirations, their expectations about their future reliance on public or private provision in different areas of their lives, we hoped that we would be able to build up a picture of what 'citizenship' might mean to them in relation to their lived experience, rather than as an abstract (or researchers') concept. Our approach cannot, however, be strictly characterised as a variant of 'grounded theory' since we were approaching these issues with far too much theoretical 'baggage' – as we have indicated in Part I. We were, nevertheless, concerned to avoid the pitfalls, also discussed in Part I, of researching citizenship by posing inappropriately direct questions formulated in the language of citizenship, which might well prove to be remote from our subjects' lived experience and the ways in which they make sense of these aspects of their lives.[1]

Contacts with those we talked to were established on a relatively informal basis. Lecturers on various courses in both universities were asked to inform their students of the general kinds of interests we had and to invite anyone who was prepared to be interviewed to make contact. We did not make a systematic attempt to create a balanced sample of students – by course, gender, age, social background or any similar variables. To some extent, indeed, our approach turned out to be a 'snowball' form of 'sampling' in that, in some cases, informal links between students led others to become involved. Having said that, our final group of respondents did contain:

- a reasonable balance between students drawn from the two universities: 18 from Cambridge and 13 from APU;
- a fair representation (across both universities) of students following vocational/prevocational programmes as compared with those following purely academic routes (this included some students following a Cambridge combined honours

course which included an Arts or Social Science component alongside the purely academic study of Education);

- a significant number of more mature students, mostly in their late twenties or thirties but with a few over 40;
- a not unreasonable gender balance given the kind of courses involved: 10 men and 21 women.

All the students were interviewed by our research assistant, Emma Creighton, using a semi-structured interview format which allowed for considerable flexibility of response by both the interviewer and the subjects. The fact that Emma was of a similar age to most of the students in the group, and had herself recently graduated from APU, facilitated ease of contact and played a crucial role in establishing an appropriately relaxed and informal atmosphere during the interviews. The average interview took about an hour – though some were rather shorter and a few considerably longer. Each interview was audio-taped and each tape was transcribed verbatim. We have identified each student by a fictitious first name and have included a brief profile of each of them in the Appendix.

It is worth pointing out that the group of students constituted in this way was in various respects 'exceptional' and not representative of the generality of higher education students across the nation. In the first place, as indicated above, we set out to include within the group a significant number of students following particular kinds of vocational and prevocational courses. Four were taking a four-year BEd degree in Cambridge and a number of others were planning to take a PGCE in the year following the interviews. At Anglia, where most students were taking various kinds of combined honours degrees, a small number included social work elements in their undergraduate programmes and others were contemplating taking postgraduate professional training courses in various social service specialisms.

Second, almost all the students were living away from home. In Cambridge some were resident in their colleges and others lived in student houses; at Anglia most were living in student houses and flats. Even among the mature students at Anglia, most had moved away from home to undertake their studies; the exceptions were certain women with both partners and children. This proportion of students living away from home is significantly higher even than the average for higher education institutions in the

Cambridgeshire and East Anglian region, and much higher than, say, in Scotland where around 90 per cent of students live in the parental home.

Third, although we did not deliberately constitute the 'sample' by reference to class or ethnic origins, the characteristics of the student intake in both the institutions in our study meant that most of those included in our group were white and broadly middle class (though as we shall see, a significant proportion drew attention to the fact that they were the first in their families to go to university).

A final type of 'exceptionalism' has to do with the 'special' characteristics of Cambridge University. This involves more than the commonplace that in terms of popular perceptions of the relative status of different UK universities 'Oxbridge' is consistently at the top. A recent comparative study by Ball *et al.* (2002) provides strong objective evidence in support of this general public perception. Interviewing students from a range of different secondary schools and 16–19 education providers, Ball *et al.* found that Cambridge and Oxford were both placed in the top four UK universities by more than 90 per cent of the students questioned in every school/16–19 college they surveyed. In those schools in the study which contained the highest proportions of pupils from social classes 1 and 2, 99–100 per cent of the students included both Cambridge and Oxford within the 'top four' (ibid.: 64).

It is also very evident from our interview data that the Cambridge University students we talked to were themselves highly conscious of the exceptional character and status of the university they were attending. Some expressed this in terms of a sense of their own good fortune and/or surprise at discovering that a *Cambridge* degree seemed to provide a passport conferring privileged access to being interviewed for high status jobs. Francesca, who was studying Economics, commented: 'One of the things that helps is that you've been to Cambridge University and I think that still matters because people will use it as a screening device and say "OK".'

A student reading Social and Political Sciences shared this perception:

> I mean, it's a Cambridge degree which I didn't really appreciate when I came here but it does help you in an incredible way. I think in some ways that stands for more than what your

actual degree is in. It gives you access to places that you don't think . . . people you can contact and stuff.

(Harriet)

Interestingly, one of our Cambridge respondents drew a direct comparison between Cambridge and APU in these respects:

Obviously I know about other people at APU and especially doing various master's degrees . . . and they're highly revered, so it's not an issue of APU being rubbish or anything like that. But I think an employer will obviously see that Cambridge University is one of the best universities.

(Kelvin)

Finally, some of the Anglia students also shared this perception and, in their cases, it played a part in their own career calculations. Sara had been accepted to read for a Cambridge MPhil degree and she explained why she had accepted this even though it would cost her more: 'It's a prestigious university . . . that's what I'm doing at Cambridge. Like I got a scholarship (for a master's course at another UK university) but I declined it because I wanted to go to Cambridge – and it cost more.'

Chapter 4

Citizenship themes in students' lives

4.1 Introduction

The purpose of our interviews with students was not to 'test' them on their political awareness or elicit their social and political philosophy. Nor did we want to ask them whether they felt themselves to be citizens in any sense. Instead we were interested in the extent to which the personal accounts of their past, present and future lives implied certain notions of society and nation. We wanted to detect any sense of national membership they might have by examining the ways they incorporated into stories of themselves, their families and their higher education, assumptions about the politics and economics of nationhood. For example, rather than asking them a whole set of direct questions about how they saw the future of state provision of health or pensions, we looked mainly at their plans after they left university and how they saw themselves managing the life course.

We report some of their responses under five themes which have significance for some of the issues raised in the preceding chapters. First, there is the question of the extent to which they see themselves as using their qualifications to detach themselves from the UK and its graduate labour market. In their accounts, to what extent did they see themselves as being 'set free' by their qualifications in a globalised world? Second, where did they see the nation in their lives and the lives of others and what sense of social rights and obligations did they have in relation to higher education? Linked to this was the third theme which questioned the extent to which they saw themselves as the private customers of higher education. Fourth, how did they see other citizens, and had their higher education constructed for them a sense of difference, distance and possibly deservedness? Finally, we look at the senses in which, mainly through informal processes, their experience of university life led to significant kinds of social and political learning, including learning from each other.

4.2 National origins but global futures?

The objective situation for the students in our group is as follows. They were just finishing their degree courses within institutions which are part of a national higher education system, funded predominantly by taxation, but one in which they or their parents have been expected to make an increasing contribution to costs (see Chapter 3). They have also been attending institutions which have, over the years, recruited numbers of students from other countries, and have been studying curricula with increasing international content taught, in many cases, by many academics who work within global professional networks. Are such conditions tending to detach students from their national origins, turning them into private consumers of and investors in a higher education which can be used anywhere? Perhaps the extreme may be represented in the vision of students buying qualifications which somehow free them from their national origins and are the means to enter global networks and markets. If high status institutions such as Cambridge University see themselves operating in international markets for research and tuition and as therefore requiring levels of funding to compete with universities in the USA and elsewhere, then it might be expected that students who obtain their qualifications here will see themselves as having an individual access to international graduate labour markets. Students attending a 'new university' like APU may not be so exposed to such globalising influences, given the recruitment of greater numbers of local students.

A persistent theme in UK higher education, in comparison with European models, has indeed been its 'de-localising' effects on young people, but for the most part this was more to secure them to the nation than propel them into international or global work. Higher proportions of students have left their parental homes for university, and this has been seen by many as an important feature of growing up and breaking away from parental dependency, a view shared by most of the younger standard entry students we interviewed. It was this feature of UK higher education

which could be seen to have made the termination of maintenance grants so significant. It may not be fanciful to say that this
de-localising had some effect on the construction of national
middle-class professional identities, even if many of those students
subsequently returned to their region or town of origin. Those
who had been away for higher education had certain claims to
have mixed with people from other communities, and while they
may not have 'seen the world', they had lived in other towns and
associated with people with other accents.

Among the younger students we interviewed there were many
who were clearly continuing this tradition of *national professionals.*
They described a standard process of applying for jobs and hopefully securing long-term employment. Those students taking a
BEd degree who we interviewed thought that, with one or two
exceptions, most of their friends were applying for teaching jobs.
Returning to one's parental home, and, in some cases, following
the career of one's parents may seem unadventurous so when Lyn
spoke of going back to teach in Norfolk and live with her mother
and father, she added that this may not be 'for ever'. She has, as
she put it 'always toyed with the idea of perhaps going abroad'.

Others had a less vocational orientation, either because of the
nature of their degree course or because their original vocational
aspirations had been changed by being at university. They
described a much less settled, predictable immediate future,
although their long-term aspirations were consistent with becoming national professionals. Anita was planning to go to Australia
for six months and work there, and had a list of things she wanted
to avoid:

> I don't want to be a social worker. Shan't do that. Never ever
> ... I don't think I want to be a police officer either because I
> did a module on that and it doesn't sound as good as I
> thought it would be. Prison service sounds quite interesting
> though. I might do that. Not sure.

Many of the students at APU, although just completing first
degrees which had vocational elements in them, were convinced
that they needed master's degrees before they could obtain professional or semi-professional employment at the level they
thought appropriate. So, despite having already incurred large
debts, they were faced with the prospect of further study and

greater indebtedness before entering work in the UK. For those who had amassed sizeable loans some mentioned the idea that they would obtain a well-paid but probably unrewarding job for a short time (Susan). Going abroad here was just an interlude, a break. While higher education had unsettled them and possibly accustomed them to a world of gaps, temporary jobs, and work experience, it was not seen as the means to a global career.

There were, however, a number of Cambridge University students with two different kinds of trajectories which did indeed project them into global networks, and these trajectories could have quite different implications for their sense of citizenship. Some might be seen as twenty-first century *missionaries* whose interests and moral commitments were applicable beyond their national boundaries, but which did not have the effect of detaching them from their origins of family and nation. Indeed, for these, it did not appear to matter where you worked, so long as the job was morally significant. Being at Cambridge University seemed to be important for these students, giving them a certain confidence, a set of contacts and perhaps even a sense of mission. Susan described some of her friends' ambitions as follows:

> Dave wants to probably do academia but he doesn't know whether he can afford it. Daphne wants to work for the UN. To be something that is connected with what she's done at Cambridge. And I know there's lots of people that want to do sort of benevolent stuff, go abroad, lots of people want to travel. Lots of people want to make a difference, I suppose. Maybe other people at other universities don't see that as being an option for them. I don't know, I might be wrong.

Harriet thought she might do a master's degree in policy but was £11,000 in debt. She wanted to work in developing countries and not settle down yet and thought she might work in Uganda. She saw herself as wanting to go into politics eventually. She had been involved in charitable projects and done voluntary work and spoke of wanting to 'effect some kind of social change' in the UK or abroad. Abigail included work in India and taking another qualification within her projections for the next two years or so. She hoped to be involved in educational projects in developing countries, but 'maybe I'll settle down and become a normal teacher one day'.

One is tempted to see, in these responses, the rudiments of a global citizenship. However, other students who also accepted that they would be likely to work away from the UK seemed to be constructing quite different future identities as *global employees*. Of great significance to their futures, as they represented them to us, was that they were about to join companies which were global operators, and while they were expecting to begin their careers with training in London, they saw themselves working in whichever global cities their employers sent them to. This was a point made with some pride. Grant was about to begin law studies sponsored by an international law firm and was keen to describe the company's global credentials:

> X is one of the so-called 'magic circle' firms, which is the sort of top five commercial firms, which employ 1400 lawyers, so it's a very big firm with, like, thirty-eight offices in forty countries ... and the beauty with a company that big is that you can get seconded out to different countries or six months' placement as part of your training.

In particular he looked forward to working in the United States:

> I've always had this inkling to work in America for a few years. I don't know, I went out there not long ago, and there's always this impression of a very sort of, they see the glass half full, whereas we see it half empty. And they do tend to be more optimistic and investors are more readily found over there, in all aspects of things really.

Internships in global cities offered by the large companies often seem to provide a first step into global employment. Luke had worked in this capacity in New York, and saw himself working in the future in such cities. Anne had been on an internship in the previous year with an American investment bank and was subsequently offered a post in their Frankfurt offices, which she was about to take up. Yet even these globalists did not see themselves at this stage as perpetually unattached and tied into mobile, corporate existence. There were doubts whether they would stay for long. Anne knew investment banking was 'a very kind of tough and demanding environment' and wondered whether she would be able to stay in it for long. Grant had a notion of 'hopping sideways' after ten years.

There is a problem for those commentators who fear the detachment of the highly educated from the nation. Concentrating on the effects of globalisation and related economic changes, they overlook some key family-based continuities which have significance for social citizenship. Writers like Reich make much of the breaks with the past but largely ignore similarities and repetitions. Both Reich and, in his different way, Lasch (1995), are very conscious of the dangers associated with the formation of a detached elite, yet they say little about the political significance of those who are also educated, and even attended the same universities, but stay behind. In the UK, at least, elite-serving universities still educate students who have a broad range of employment destinies, including the lower nationally-based professions. In Reich's approach, those who enter such occupations are termed the 'in-person servers', who appear as both at risk and somehow inactive. Instead it may be possible to see them more positively as occupied in maintaining and even reconstructing the nation at home.

In their conversations with us the students in our group provided much evidence of continuities with the past, with their higher education continuing to perform its traditional national, social functions as far as their families were concerned. Most of these students saw themselves using their qualification to enter occupations which were not only within their nation of origin but also had some social significance. Because of the content of the degrees of the people we interviewed, there was perhaps inevitably a clear preference for jobs in either the state bureaucracies or non-profit-making organisations. Finance, law, publishing, human resources and management consultancy were the few areas being considered in the private sector.

And for those becoming national professionals, higher education was also still playing the traditional role as a key mechanism of social class mobility and class maintenance. For many of them it was clear that an important part of their sense of self was as the first in their family to go to university, yet coming from families whose members might have gone if circumstances had been different:

> I'm the first person of my family to go into higher education. My grandfather could have gone into higher education but he grew up between the wars and during the depression and

there wasn't the money. I mean, he was qualified to go but the money just wasn't there. So, erm, the family has always put a great stress on education. But even so, I'm still the first to go on to university.

(Andy)

The stories of their families are told in terms of fathers, mothers and grandparents who had abilities but were frustrated. 'University didn't enter the equation. Both my parents were working-class people' (Jasmine). There was a father who was good at art but came from a large family and never had a chance (Lydia) and a mother whose parents saved to send her to a private school but who became pregnant. There were also students who were carrying on their family's tradition of public employment and public service and this appeared to involve a transmission not only of employment orientation but also social political sentiments. A number of BEd students had one or both parents in teaching.

In the accounts of origins and destinations by the global employees and missionaries, there were interesting continuities too. On the surface they seemed to be the representatives of a new globalised world, rootless individuals constructing their futures on a world stage. In fact, most were continuing family traditions, and many were using family money to do so. Both the missionaries and the global employees accounted for their great confidence by referring to fact that Cambridge had provided them with a universally acknowledged qualification of value, contacts with a range of diverse people, and experience of activities that would in their view not have been available elsewhere. Yet, in their biographies there were many other, family-based experiences which could be no less significant – living in other countries, and family-funded gap years which included extensive travel. For some their lives were already de-nationalised, coming to Cambridge from other European countries, or having parents who worked abroad and whose financial assets were substantial and easily transferable. Both Anne's parents were graduates who had themselves attended universities in different countries.

4.3 The nation in their lives: the students' sense of social rights and obligations

Clearly, for those who came to the UK to study, the connection between their sense of the nation and their higher education experience would be indirect. In fact coming from another country did appear to have stimulated them to think about the role of the state as far as higher education was concerned. It is obvious from the following how, for some families and students, the current relationships between family, nation, citizenship and higher education are confusing. Anne had substantial financial support from her parents and grandparents in Germany as well as access to a small scholarship fund. However, she was well aware of the fact that, coming from an EU country, she only paid tuition at the level of British students: 'And basically I'm incredibly grateful to the British state because I can come here for the same money that English students can come.'

When Marco first came from Italy he was surprised that English universities were free. And when fees and loans replaced grants he thought it was wrong: 'But on the other hand I do think that £1,000 for what you get here in England isn't much compared to universities in Europe ... I think there's quite good support from the government.'

Abigail was technically an overseas student because her parents were resident in Switzerland, although they had owned a house in the UK on which they paid Council Tax. Yet she was herself a British citizen. As far as paying for higher education, she saw herself as a 'private' student, being charged full tuition fees because Switzerland was not in the EU. She estimated the total cost of her degree would be £32,000, of which £9,000 was money she earned and the rest was from her parents, and she only expected to have a small debt. She found it upsetting that fellow students who did not hold a British passport yet whose parents lived in an EU country could pay so little.

For young UK students there was also much confusion. This seemed to arise, not from definitions of national entitlement but from the way the current policy works for young people, who are constructed as partly dependent upon their families and partly as individual loan borrowers (Ahier, 2000). They all knew exactly how much they were borrowing as individuals. Most thought they would end with a debt of between £6,000 and £10,000. But they also reported on the close involvement of their parents, and, again, most knew exactly how much their parents or other relatives would have contributed to their higher education by the end of their courses. This was partly because their parents were usually paying for identifiable items such as rent and food, which had been agreed as their responsibility when the students first went to university.

However, most of these students were very perplexed about the nature of public, state support for their higher education. Exactly what the state, or other tax-payers or society contributed remained shrouded in mystery. There was a suspicion that the state was paying somewhere, but when they talked of costs the discussion was dominated by the day-to-day calculations of savings being used up, part-time earnings, parents' contributions, and debts being amassed. Only five of this group mentioned the public costs of tuition and only two made a reasonably informed estimate:

> Students just pay £1,050 I think, isn't it, but the government fills in the rest of the £5,000 or whatever it is per year. So I think it's probably public spending mainly. Not mine because I don't pay tax.
>
> (Anita)

Emily had deferred entry to her course by a year and was thus still receiving a grant and paid no tuition fees. She could not understand the current arrangements but had the feeling that 'if they're making individuals pay more, then the public must logically be paying less, but I'm not sure if that's true ... So without any knowledge I would say that the individuals are the ones who are suffering.'

It was interesting that of the very few who acknowledged public costs, two (Emily and Philip) were deferred-entry students who were therefore not expected to pay for tuition. In a way and ironically, introducing means-tested tuition fees may have the effect of hiding the sizeable public contribution.

If so many of these students see themselves and their families as the main purchasers of their higher education, how do they see their links with the state in the future? If any *rights* they might have had to a free higher education have become compromised by loans, fees and means-testing, do they think they have any *obligations* in this area, other than to pay back the loans? Certainly paying back their student loan is taken seriously by most of them, and in some cases is a significant part of their medium-term future life-plans. Melanie, envisaging a loan of £9,000, thought that the kind of work she really wanted to do would not be sufficient to pay off the loan. For three years, therefore, she thought that she might work in 'a well-paid job that doesn't do necessarily massive amounts for my creative outlets, or whatever, just to earn the money'. Susan who had just completed a section of the Social and Political Science Tripos and was about to begin a Part II in veterinary clinical practice, saw a period in veterinary general practice as the means of paying back the loan:

> So that's when I want to concentrate on paying off the loans and get them paid off as soon as I can. So, yeah, hopefully get the loans all paid off in like two or three years and then, sort of, then think about what I really want to do for the rest of the time.

Paying back parents was not considered. She thought that: 'Helping your children is just what parents do. You don't expect anything back.' Others, however, did refer to obligations to the family, though sometimes with a certain levity: 'I think my parents will expect me to keep them in a life they've become accustomed to or something when I'm older' (Harriet). In similar vein, Margaret said that her parents were joking when they told her, 'We've invested all this money in you and we're hoping to get a return on it.'

For the younger students there was an awareness of a debt to parents, the scale of which was often equated with their parents' loss of holidays, and many thought it was unfair that parents were expected to pay instead of the government. However, whenever they mentioned a duty to give back to parents what they had given to them, perhaps when old, they quickly added that their parents were not expecting it:

> My mother told me quite often she doesn't expect me to do anything for them. But I mean, I want to if I can.
>
> (Emily)

> I would always love to be able to support them in a way, and kind of do a bit ... sort of pay them back for some of the

huge thousands of millions of pounds they've put into me, you see. But they're not expecting it.

(Denise)

When it came to discussions about paying back to *society*, many rejected any notion of obligation. The feeling was that if you paid for your degree then, as a graduate, you had no such special responsibilities. As one student expressed it, 'You do a degree for yourself really' (Marco), and others made the point thus: 'I mean, considering we're all having to pay for . . . having to pay for your own tuition fees, I don't think you have to give anything back to society' (Samantha). Samantha thought that if the state had paid for your degree then you would have an obligation, but '. . . we live in a free world. You're free to make your own choices.' For Jasmine, any paying back to society was just impractical because:

> Companies are now so global that you can't restrict yourself to one country. I think they [graduates] ought to start here, but then it may lead to jobs elsewhere and you can't say no to it because you feel obliged to stay in the country you were educated in. Lots of people come to this country but they've never been educated here, so it works both ways.

For those who thought graduates had some wider obligations, there were differences about how these could be fulfilled. Most future state employees thought they fulfilled their wider obligations by actually working for the state. For example, two students who were about to begin teaching thought they were paying society back through their occupation:

> Well, I feel I'm doing my share of paying back by becoming a teacher really.

(Helen)

> My job will be doing enough for the children of Britain.

(Anne)

Those who saw themselves working for charities or voluntary bodies also shared such notions. A 'missionary' (Denise) thought graduates should 'get a decent job so you should be paying decent tax back' but she herself was 'going into something that actually helps society'. She spoke with some despair about those entering banking who were not going to help anyone. She was also the only student to articulate the classic citizenship justification for higher education – providing the means to become politically informed:

> I think we've got that kind of responsibility, to be that group of people, you know, ... and not just the middle classes, but y'know to be that group of people who understand and who are intelligent and kind of use it in a constructive way rather than just make themselves money.

Those entering private companies also saw the point of making this kind of distinction between working in 'public service' and elsewhere. Although she was herself going to work in a bank, and had an economics degree, Francesca thought that the state had been generous, but acknowledged that:

> in some subjects you can probably give a lot more back than in others. Because if you're doing medicine and then you work for the NHS, then I think you're really giving back. But if you go and do economics and go and work for a bank maybe it's a bit difficult. Though you probably can through taxes.

Carolyn, who was thinking about public relations and event management, described the idea of 'giving something back' to society as follows:

> Well, I think if people like what they are doing and they are good at it, they'll inevitably give something back to society, because they'll excel, and in that case they'll be able to do more. So in my case, if it's event organisation, and I can really produce good parties, and people enjoy them, and that's the business, then not only will I have more money to give back to society ... in the form of tax, and in the form of contributions as well, you know. I'll personally have more choice about what charities I give money to, and how much. And then, you know, people will be happier.

What did these students consider to be their future rights and obligations beyond higher education? They certainly seem to share an expectation of further privatisation, though many felt very ambivalent about this. On the one hand, a clear majority expressed high levels of support *in principle* for a continuing framework of welfare benefits free at the point of delivery and available as of right to all but the 'undeserving'. If few were as outspoken as Peter, who was unabashed in declaring that 'there should be a strong welfare state and Socialism's only dead on paper', many more seemed to feel strongly that the state should continue to fund primary and secondary schooling, the National Health Service, basic pensions, unemployment benefit for those able and willing to search for employment, and so on. Moreover, not a few were scathing about what they saw as the inadequate levels of certain existing provisions – such as the Minimum Wage: Anne, for example, commented, 'What is it, £3.60 an hour? That's pathetic isn't it?' Francesca expressed similarly strong reservations about what she saw as the stigma attaching to various means-tested benefits: 'People should have their dignity to be able to live dignified lives and not have to ask for things.'

In spite of such principled support, however, many looked forward with at best a mixture of apprehension and uncertainty to a future in which benefits could well be increasingly eroded. Discussing health care, Samantha worried that 'If you think of how the UK and the NHS compares with the US where you have to *pay* for health care, I mean, to have to do that would be a nightmare' and she comforted herself with a less than fully confident feeling that 'hopefully it won't come to that'. The majority, though, seemed resigned to the *inevitability* of further privatisation, not as an emergent principle with which they agreed but as a tendency through which they were living. Partly as a result of their own experience of the loans and fees issues, it is as though they saw themselves at the end of state benevolence. Helen catches perfectly this sense of an irreversible drift in which she felt caught up:

HELEN: I think perhaps with the way things I can see are going, we'd need to try and get some private health cover.
INTERVIEWER: How do you feel about that?
HELEN: Well, I think it's probably just inevitable. It's how it seems to be going. Perhaps it can be avoided but I feel that if you can sort of pay your own way that is the way we seem to be encouraged to be going.

Similarly, Kelvin emphasised that 'private health is not something I necessarily agree with but I think it's something . . . that'll figure within the next ten years'. Kelvin also mentioned 'the growing emphasis on private *pensions*', something that was amplified by Jonathan, one of the oldest students in our sample, who suggested that the growing problems surrounding employer-based pension schemes might actually produce an *increase* in those relying on state benefits:

> There's still a lot of elderly people that only have state pension and there may be a greater number coming into retirement with state and employer pensions but with all the changes that are coming in . . . where they're doing away with final salary schemes – BT's bringing in these share pension schemes where you're tied to the market – so I think in the future there's going to be an awful lot of people that will be relying on benefits. They're just not going to get what they hoped to get I think.

Despite this clear sense of the problems of using private provision to insure against risk, Jonathan nevertheless seemed to think changes of this sort were inevitable.

For some in our group, perhaps especially those who felt confident of earning high salaries, this unfolding of a general social tendency towards private provision and the anticipated trajectory of their own lives, coincided. Within this broader context, their principled support for public services was qualified in their own cases by doubts about the quality of the services that might be available. Several foresaw themselves 'exiting' from public provision if the need arose. Francesca felt she was very likely to exercise certain options of this kind though she also thought this would not be possible for the majority:

> If I had children they might use state education, at least for primary education. I'm not sure about the NHS because, yeah, I'd probably go on using that for a bit unless I have something I was worried about or there was a long waiting list, then I'd probably go private. In general, I do think I'd probably use the private sector more in the long run . . . But I think the vast majority of people will go on using the state sector.

Philip described a different quality dilemma – but the underlying
message about 'exit where necessary' was the same: 'with people,
like, in inner city schools . . . if the quality continues to be like shit
. . . people are faced with a problem, you know, that they don't
want their kids going there so I think they will be making more of
a shift towards like private education in those areas'. Such feelings
seemed, in some cases, to have been reinforced by a belief that
public sector employment would inevitably continue to be a 'poor
relation' compared to the private sector, with the implication that
this would contribute to an inexorable decline in quality. Harriet
commented:

> I think there's a problem with that kind of employment . . . I
> know as part of teaching recruitment they're giving them a
> £6,000 bursary, and things like social workers, I mean it's a
> very difficult job and they get an incredibly bad press. I think
> they're going to have problems across the board, in local
> government and all those kind of issues. They are the not-for-
> profit sector.

The alternatives to state provision and state dependency may be
taken to be either continued dependence upon their families,
which was generally rejected, or making use as consumers of the
financial services, in the form of private health insurance,
employment protection, loans, private education, etc. Although
few admitted to knowing anything much about such things, they
generally seemed quite confident as future consumers of such
financial products. As Carolyn put it: 'If I need a pension, I'll go
and find out how to set up a pension.' In many important
respects these young people were convinced that they *would* have
to make private provision, and their future well-being would
indeed be in many ways up to them. This orientation to self-
provision often went hand in hand with rejecting any sense of a
community of economic fate, and a belief that the most important determinants of their futures were their own efforts, or, if
they saw themselves entering private sector careers, the company
they worked for. Luke presented a view of future fortunes as
combined in an identity of the enterprising self. He saw himself
with a mortgage and health insurance in the next few years, and
when asked what he saw as most affecting his financial future he
replied:

I would say at first my career, so the organisation that employs me. But I think more how I manage my own funds. I imagine if I was going to make money I'd have to be investing it in things and going for shares . . . I've done a bit of investing.

It was only those who saw themselves working for the state who admitted that how the national economy went might prove to be crucial: 'The economy has got to be the big thing. Because if the economy's screwed you don't have the jobs to go into. And it doesn't matter whether you have a degree or not' (Melanie).

4.4 Customers, investors and consumers

The arguments that introducing loans and tuition fees would make students into active, cost-conscious customers of higher education institutions seeking value for money, receive little support in these students' reflections. Only one raised such issues as far as tuition was concerned, and this was as much a political reaction as a customer's complaint. Harriet acknowledged that the public purse still paid for most of the costs of higher education, even after tuition fees had been introduced, but wondered where the extra money actually went:

I mean a lot of the money that obviously goes into universities and their libraries and their facilities and their academics and stuff but I mean I haven't had a very quality degree to be honest. I think the quality of my education has been crap . . . At the moment the balance in university is not directed towards students. The balance is totally orientated towards research especially with your Research Assessment Exercise, and I just think, if they're going to increase the cost for a student, then the switch has to be back towards students.

When the university was told to improve their efficiency, the bills of students whack up and it's just, like, we don't come first. Like the research comes first. Do you know what I mean? Teaching is secondary and that's not what it's supposed to be 'cos like I mean I'm £11,000 in debt and, like, which is a lot of money.

Similarly Tony looked back and acknowledged how committed his tutors had been, but confessed to a certain disappointment; 'It ain't great, it ain't perfect, but then that's underfunding for you.'

The students' general lack of customer consciousness in relation to their higher education could be approached from a
number of different directions, and again, we found the private,
family links to be important. First, in the case of standard entry
students, their actual sources of money were diverse, and, in
many cases, it was difficult to say exactly who was paying. In the
case of these younger students their families were intimately
involved, paying their rent, for example, or giving them money
towards incidental expenses. In other, related research, we have
found that such arrangements reflect the relative abilities of
parents to pay and also their own experiences of higher education
(Ahier 2001). Because the costs incurred and paid for privately
were chiefly those of rent, travel and food, it was these costs which
were associated in the students' minds primarily with higher education as a process of growing up and learning independence,
and less with gaining specific skills or knowledge for use later.
These more general developmental benefits were felt to be
obtained almost regardless of tuition and content, by a process of
making friends, meeting, mixing and talking. They were not
subject to calculation. Only two students transformed these
unspecific benefits into useful capital. Harriet mentioned this
process as gaining 'contacts', the supposed lifeblood of global
networks from an individual's point of view, and Denise said she
had 'learned kind of people management skills as well as just
friendship'.

It was this same attachment to the non-specific, personal benefits of higher education which also seemed to restrict their
approach to it as an investment. Philip, who was completing a
Cambridge economics degree, did acknowledge that one acquires
specific analytical skills on such a course, and that gives you access
to a certain group of well-paid jobs. He described the course as a
'kind of almost a finishing school for, like, investment bankers
and management consultants'. Yet even he, when talking about
the benefits of the degree as far as he was concerned, described
them as meeting people from a wide range of backgrounds, and
being forced to justify your opinions in informal discussions about
political matters. Others, doing social science degrees at APU
where, perhaps, the employment benefits may not be so direct,
were aware of credential inflation, and accepted that they needed
a degree to enter jobs which could have been done with A levels
in the past. As Andy put it, 'OK, there aren't, you know, not many

jobs that I could apply for now, with this degree, but if I didn't do the degree, there'd be, like, even less opportunity.'

Turning now to so-called *non*-standard-entry students, the situation proved to be not so different. Older students at Anglia mentioned how they were restricted in their previous employment by the lack of a degree, but none were intending to return to their previous area of employment and they did not see their degree as an investment with obvious economic returns. Indeed, some saw themselves in a worse position economically. Laura had been working in a bank since she was 16 but after three years studying sociology wanted to be a research assistant. She thought that she would be worse off:

> Well, put it like this, if I get a job as a research assistant I'll be earning less than I was before I graduated so I'm certainly not doing it for the money. Three years older three years wiser and with a degree!

One might have expected that, for older students, the links between costs and benefits would have been more open to calculation. Not only would they be less enmeshed in their families of origin, they would also be unlikely to have entered higher education to gain independence, or to grow up. It is possible that in such cases, getting a qualification may be more of a calculation about investing in new skills. And it is true that the students in this situation *were* very conscious of the costs of funding their higher education from their own individual savings, earnings and loans. Jasmine, when considering her own circumstances, acknowledged that it had cost her between £30,000 and £40,000 what with earnings forgone, travel expenses and so on. Others described a whole set of sources of money: overdrafts, savings, insurance policies, cashing in premium bonds, as well as part-time work. However, even these students were often dependent upon others. For example, Tony, who was aged 30, spoke of combining a maximum loan and part-time work with 'hand-outs' from parents and two small inheritances. A number also mentioned substantial help from husbands and partners and ex-partners. Laura talked of 'subsidies' from her husband, combined with a loan of £8,000, an overdraft and part-time employment. The costs of studying were in these ways incorporated into the complexities of domestic money. Lydia had a partner who was an engineer. He continued to pay the mortgage and had now taken on all the bills which had previously been shared.

These mature students who were so aware of the actual costs to them as individuals often saw their higher education as a way of escaping their past and entering a new life. In terms used by other researchers of mature students, their accounts of entering higher education were narratives of 'unfulfilled potential' and 'self-transformation', not 'credentialism' (Britton and Baxter 1999). It was interesting that some actually made a contrast between the instrumentalism of their earlier education and their higher education. Laura thought that her degree had made her less naïve and able to make sense of the newspapers, which was where her schooling had failed:

> I think when I was at school, I did my GCSEs and I did them through memory. And my parents really had the view of education in that you do your exams just for the purpose of getting a job. Which is really what I did.

Andy's life story is a perfect illustration of this orientation to higher education among some older students. He had originally failed to obtain good enough A levels to go to university when he left school. This he saw as setting him on a conventional life course, working in local government. It was 'just a case of get a job, earn money, get married, have kids'. Doing a degree later was part of the enterprise of changing his life, with the major benefit bringing what he saw as heightened self-esteem, 'which was sadly lacking after working in the public sector for so long'. In all such accounts the identity of customer or investor would be quite alien.

Other aspects of investment consciousness were missing or explicitly rejected as applicable to HE by both the young and the older students. They did not seem to have considered issues of risk; very few thought of opportunities forgone; and they did not favour a higher education system in which the more money you put in the better your returns. They all saw differential fees or 'top-up fees', which were being discussed in the newspapers at the time, as very unfair – and a number doing Cambridge University degrees maintained they would not have paid more had such fees been in place when they applied. Some associated differential fees with a programme of changing student consciousness. Andy, a self-confessed 'dyed in the wool socialist', saw differential fees as 'commercialism': 'What they're trying to do is to set up a premier league, in that sense so they make people pay for the brand name with no guarantes of a better product.' Luke could see that the effects would be to turn students into calculators and consumers: 'And if you're talking about top-up fees, you're definitely going to have to look at it and see what you do get out of it, look at it as a bit of a commodity.'

Only Philip thought differential fees made some sense, partly because he thought it odd that parents of those students who had sent them to private schools were actually paying significantly less to send them to Cambridge. However, he saw problems for the less well off and thought differential fees would have to be 'tempered' by hardship funds.

As far as these students are concerned, then, there must be some doubt about the success of the original political project of turning university students from state dependants into individual customers and investors. However, we *have* found evidence that the system of loans was accentuating the identity of students as consumers of a lifestyle which was highly differentiated by their access to money. The former grant system did produce a certain uniformity among students – by providing a standardising sum which all students were meant to receive, whether from the state, or from parents if they were well off, or from a combination of the two. (One of the arguments for loans at the time they were introduced, was that students who had rich but parsimonious parents could, independently, borrow money to make up the shortfall (Barr 1989).) In recent research, however, there is substantial evidence of spiralling individual student debt combined with consumerist lifestyles (UNITE 2002) and some of our group described a situation where high expenditure went with support from generous parents and also with a range of debts. Delphine's parents had paid the rent, she had money from the access fund, an £8,000 student loan, had 'dipped into' bank loans, and worked part-time. There have always been rich and poor students but the current situation could be seen as corrosive of any student-citizen solidarity. And in a hot-house of student consumerism, it may be not surprising that students from less favoured backgrounds are borrowing more than others, just to keep up. Not only that, but with the exception of those who may not have access to family money which might be used to repay the loans, it is clear that such a large degree of indebtedness prior to entering full-time employment is hardly likely to provide much sense of economic independence. Many of the students we interviewed were well aware of this in the way they described their futures as consumers and employees, where the servicing of debt was seen as a long-term commitment and just part of life. When they talked about their financial futures they envisaged an uninterrupted move from completing their loan repayments to taking out a mortgage, because this was the only means of entering a property-owning democracy.

For those contemplating a second degree the prospect appears even more daunting. Sara saw herself finishing her higher education with a second loan added to her current one of £8,000. She thought herself fortunate to come from an Asian family whom she expected to help with repayments and provide accommodation when she began work. On the way her father was going to pay the fees for her second degree she said: 'I don't mind him paying because at the end of the day, for us, in our Asian communities, you know, we think we are our father's, not property, but responsibility until whatever time.'

The problem is that for those students without family assets and support, the policies aimed at producing positive active entrepreneurial citizens are also likely to produce anxious, dominated consumers, who have been obliged to swap reliance upon the state for dependence on the financial services. UNITE's Student Living Report when surveying the full range of university students, found both greater investment and customer orientation than we did, but this was combined with high levels of stress (UNITE 2002: 11.2).

4.5 Other citizens

We have seen that, at least as undergraduates, these students did not tend to see themselves as individual customers and investors in self. Many were, in a sense, collectivised via dependence upon their families, and for the most part they see their futures within their nation's boundaries. But how does the society to which they belong seem to them? In particular, how are others within that same society perceived, and how important is the status of graduate in constructing any differences between themselves and these others? We asked no direct questions about their beliefs on class and inequality but it was clear from accounts of their pasts and futures where certain crucial social divisions existed for these students.

None of our interviewees attempted to use explicit cultural judgements to sustain distinctions between graduate and non-graduate. If they thought that they had no particular obligations as graduates (see above), they also struggled with the idea that graduates may have any particular rights. Interestingly, however, some did attempt to articulate their access, as graduates, to better jobs and more money as a form of property rights:

> Mm, I do think that if you've studied for something then, yes, you do deserve the right to earn more because you have worked for that area. But then in certain instances what you go on to do is nothing related to your degree but the fact that you've sort of invested a lot of your own personal time and invested a lot of your money into bettering yourself, educationally, perhaps, yes, we do deserve a bit more.
>
> (Helen)

> I've really worked really hard so I think that should be rewarded in some way. You know, a certain recognition through status of career, salary perhaps. Obviously it's difficult because you always do come back to the Cambridge thing, you know, and certainly I think you earn the right here to be respected, well, because of the place, because obviously you've come to Cambridge, you know, obviously the degree is highly revered, therefore you earn the right to be respected within the workplace.
>
> (Kelvin)

Others, while expecting higher salaries as a result of their qualification, expressed some uneasiness about the notion of graduates' rights on various grounds. Some saw themselves as privileged to have had the opportunities, and had doubts anyway that differential rewards in our society were based on usefulness:

> I would probably feel even more strongly that you don't have any particular rights because it would be people that had already had certain privileges that got to do the degree ... I don't think it gives them rights because they have certain privileges in the first place.

Rights are very difficult. Well, in some ways I do expect a better salary but I, erm, that's the way the world works and I want a better salary so I got a degree but I don't think that salary structure really reflects how useful people are.

(Lydia)

Many were suspicious of graduates declaring their rights to greater rewards without being prepared to work hard for them. Because they doubted that their higher education had given them specific skills for use in employment, they generally accepted the idea that those who do not enter higher education but had gained lengthy work experience should be rewarded at the same level as themselves.

There were, however, *some* crucial implied social distinctions being made within these discussions. Given the way both the younger and older students had described the personal and private benefits of going to university, one may expect them to have reservations about non-graduates, if not as employees then as people with whom they would associate. 'I can't think of anyone I know that isn't doing a degree, or done a degree', said Susan, and in talk about their future social and economic lives it was clear that most were expecting to enter communities made up almost exclusively of graduates:

INTERVIEWER: Do you think your circle of friends in the future will mostly include graduates?
MELANIE: Erm, thinking ahead in the short term, yes, because I suppose there'll be people who I'm working with, they'll all be graduates. And the main circle of my friends at the moment will have all done degrees, and my boyfriend and his friends will have had to do degrees for their jobs as well.

Some spoke of an indeterminate fellowship of graduates:

Sometimes, it sounds really weird, but it seems when you speak to another graduate, you're just on the same wave-length. Whereas I speak to some school friends that didn't go on to university and they just seem to have different priorities, objectives. You just can't have a good conversation with them. And, yeah, it's just a different outlook.

(Sara)

Other research has identified the notion of being *destined* to go to university among certain young sixth-formers (Pugsley 1998; Ahier 2001; Ball *et al*. 2002) and these undergraduates, in turn, were now seeing themselves as *the kinds of people* who became graduates:

> I took a year out before school and university and I did think about not coming to university at all. And one of my friends said to me, 'Oh don't be silly, people like you always go to university.' And it was just kind of assumed ... there is a kind of feeling of ease, if someone goes to university, it's, like, that's the social norm.
>
> (Carolyn)

We know little about the wider social functions of graduation in societies where a third or more of school leavers go to university. Given the way recruitment into higher education still favours the middle class (Metcalf 1997; Williams 1997; Forsyth and Furlong 2000; Ball *et al*. 2002), 'being a graduate' may now act not only as the means to enter professional and managerial employment but may also be coming to constitute the minimum entry requirement for middle-class friendships and partnerships. With the emergence of so-called assortative mating, where partners now tend to have similar qualifications and earnings thereby accentuating household differences in income (Lasch 1995: 33), the socio-economic functions of higher education may need to be reconsidered. One or two students, particularly the older ones at APU, were conscious of the way they might be sounding snobbish. Peter thought that having graduate friends was down to chance:

> I'm certainly not going to just go out of my way to seek out graduate friends and say, 'Oh hi! I like the tie. Where's that from?' No, not at all. If it happens it will be a coincidence.

Most students in our group did, however, make certain social distinctions *among their fellow students*. Some of these were based on playful generalisations referring to style, related to gender and/or the subject studied. Anne claimed that arts students tend to have larger book shelves: 'Oh yes, they have all sorts of books, whereas science students have kind of larva lamps, that kind of thing.'

One division, however, was much more serious and appeared

time and again within the interviews of students at Cambridge University, and may have arisen because of the way some companies recruit graduates from such high status institutions regardless of the content of their degrees. This division was constructed around differences not in origins, but in destinations. It was between those students who were destined for what might be broadly termed public service and those others who were entering what were seen as highly rewarded occupations associated with banking, finance and investment, for which the shorthand term used was 'going into the City'. It is difficult to clarify the exact basis of these views. Students who saw themselves moving into careers in areas such as social work, teaching, and research did seem to imply that others, studying the same degree, seeking wealth in the private sector, were personally and culturally different, and this applied particularly to those entering the finance industry. They themselves said they did not think too much about money, and knew that their wages would be low in comparison. Yet they did have a sense of unfairness, fed by the suspicion that the skills of those people going into the financial services were not essentially different from their own. Indeed, some of those identified as entering such employment were doing the same courses as those moving into the state professions, and it may have been difficult for them to recognise the qualities which were to be rewarded so disproportionately.

To some this awareness of other people's earnings may seem just the expression of petty-minded, class-sector envy. For those entering the labour market with no post-school qualifications, the starting salaries spoken about by these undergraduates, whether entering the private *or* public sectors, could seem like nothing to complain about. Furthermore, the starting salaries mentioned by almost all of our interviewees were actually the average salary for all graduates which, in the year in which our interviews were conducted, was £14,200 (IES 2001). However, it is possible that these perceptions – which in many cases relate to earning prospects further along different typical career paths – may have long-term implications for social citizenship.

As we have noted above, there was a tendency for some of the younger students to follow their parents into the state professions, particularly teaching. We have found that in many such cases, their parents have attempted to support their children by giving them the equivalent of the grant which they themselves had received from the state (Ahier 2001). Until recently this has been made possible by a combination of secure employment, rising house prices and favourable investment and savings conditions. Any change in these circumstances, however, could have the effect of producing an even more envious (or at least resentful), disassociated, and self-recruiting sector of graduate public service employees. Harriet expressed the predicament of those who come from public service families and use their degrees to enter similar employment. She acknowledged that 'the kind of work I want to go into, the wages are crap', and went on to express outrage at the starting salaries expected by many other Cambridge graduates:

> All the people I know who are going into investment and management, they are all starting on at least £25,000, like, and so many people are earning more money than my mum, and my mum's, like, a head teacher and she's spent thirty years working towards that goal.

As we argued in Chapter 3, the interests of state employees, such as university lecturers or school teachers, must be distinguished from wider considerations of social citizenship. Yet the morale of public servants *is* important for maintaining the services upon which such citizenship currently depends. And in view of this, it may be important as suggested above, that the status of graduate may play a part in enabling members of the middle class to find private solutions to certain of the problems of social reproduction. The work of Savage *et al.* (1992: 154–7) on the way middle-class households commonly combine a range of assets, suggests ways in which private and public employment can, in some cases, be used in the same family – and some of the students hinted at these possibilities. For example, Anne, who was to be a teacher, saw her partner's job as likely to give her and her future family access to private medicine.

The key issue is whether these students could see any *public* ways out of the dilemma – which appears to them in the following way. They are borrowing large amounts of money to obtain a given degree which is necessary for *any* of the occupations they may enter. Their rewards, however, seem to depend, not on their success in the degree, or their espousal of the loftier purposes of higher education, but upon whether they enter certain sectors of private enterprise or enter public service. Some noted that the situation is even more problematic because many public service jobs required additional qualifications for which they had to go further into debt. With all-graduate professions now dominating these public services, there are only a limited number of ways out. For example, taxes could be raised so that there might be both some redistribution of the rewards to graduation between the public and private, and greater use of public funds to finance higher education itself. Another approach may be to accentuate the differences between the costs of degrees so that those destined for public employment might pay less for a cheaper, perhaps shorter higher education.

The students we interviewed seemed to accept the inevitability of tax resistance and, as we have seen, most were resigned to continuing privatisation of public services which they and others were currently receiving free. Yet they were also set against any differentiation of higher education by cost. As we have also noted, during the period of the interviews, so-called top-up fees were being promoted by some university vice-chancellors but their students – at least judging from the reactions of our group – were quite opposed to them. For example, Peter thought differential fees were 'dangerous', and he saw them as part of a trend: 'People that can afford a better education will, and then everyone else will get left behind with the supposedly crappy universities.'

Most, though, saw it as inevitable that it would be the well off who would go to the expensive high status institutions and they had no doubt that this *would* happen. Kelvin thought that if a Cambridge degree gave you more money, people would pay more for it. Grant acknowledged that most people were against it but would go along: the benefits of going to an expensive institution would outweigh what he called the 'moral stance'. As we have already seen, Helen typically combined a view of the inexorable ongoing privatisation of services with a stance, shared by all except one of the other students, that was set against 'top-up fees'. Despite this acceptance of the apparent inevitability of further privatisation, however, she like some others felt that she would not have paid extra to come to Cambridge:

> If I had to pay extra to come to Cambridge I wouldn't have done it. I mean when I applied here I didn't really see myself as coming to Cambridge and having an advantage over

people and I seriously considered going elsewhere ... So if
they had said come here and pay extra or go elsewhere, I
would have gone elsewhere.

4.6 Educating each other: peer discussion and political awareness

In previous sections we have drawn attention to certain significant
divisions among our group of respondents, notably between those
destined for 'City' employment and those entering a range of
public service occupations. On the other hand, we also noted the
existence of a surprisingly high level of consensus across the
whole group that policies such as tuition fees and top-up fees were
objectionable in principle on grounds which many identified as
'moral'.

Although the making explicit of such views was elicited via the
artificial situation of a research interview, it was nevertheless
evident that for many in our group, going to university *was* seen as
having significantly changed their outlooks, enlarged their political awareness, and enhanced their self-confidence. We are aware,
of course, of the problems of interpreting such claims. It is, after
all, something of a cliché that students always say that they learn
more from their peers than from their courses, and it is also the
case that young people still in the process of maturing may view
the transformative effects of university as more far-reaching than
in many cases they turn out to be. Despite such reservations,
however, we believe our evidence does suggest that for many of
those we talked to, an important part of their university lives was
that they found themselves engaged in a significant process of
mutual social learning that included 'political' learning. This
often occurred through interaction with their peers, but also
through more complex circuits in which ideas encountered in
their courses entered into peer discussion and contributed both
to the widening of their political horizons and also to a greater
self-confidence in their capacity to reflect about broadly political
issues in more informed ways.

We have already mentioned one significant dimension of this:
the fact that various government policies were directly impacting
on their lives raised the consciousness even of those who confessed that generally speaking they were politically uninformed
and uninvolved. Emily, who candidly admitted, 'I bury my head

in the sand and don't read any newspapers', nevertheless remarked:

> I used to be, well, quite Conservative really but I've become a lot less Conservative over the last three years. And it's mostly from just seeing my friends and the problems they've had to deal with from the government and what they've been doing with the funding.

Similarly, Anne commented:

> I know a lot more about politics than I did and my views have definitely changed. At school you're not directly in line at all. Yet at university, things like top-up fees or cutting student grants, it has actually affected me directly and it has affected my bank account literally. So a lot more things apply to you rather than it just being on the news. So I think I now know far more about it.

Others who confessed to having been similarly uninterested in politics before going to university spoke of a broader, though certainly not 'deep', process of becoming more politically aware. Margaret, for example, contrasted her almost total political ignorance and lack of involvement before coming to university with her current attitude: 'Now I at least make the effort to read their manifestos and vote'. Significantly, she added: 'A lot of it, I think, is being with other people from all different areas.'

This theme – bringing together the effects of moving away from home often to a different part of the country, living on a day-to-day basis with a broader range of people with different social and geographical origins, and its broadening effect on social and political awareness – was repeatedly emphasised by our respondents. Kelvin speaks for many when he observes: 'You see a lot of people here. It's almost like a melting pot. Especially from different parts of the country as well, and so I've definitely been influenced by other people's opinions.'

For many, this exposure to a greater diversity of people and viewpoints than they had previously encountered was closely linked to a sense of growing self-confidence and a conviction that their social skills had grown as their networks of friends and acquaintances had widened. Denise contrasted her less confident former self with the person she had now become: 'I used to look at jobs and things and say, "I couldn't do *that*, that's like for people up there" . . . but now I think, "well, actually I *could* do that if I put my mind to it" '. And Harriet, who had devoted much of her time at university to fund-raising activities for overseas charities, felt the same way: 'I've become much more independent, do you know, like meeting people from different charities and stuff like that, we've held lots of presentations from different charities and you learn how to operate and get in touch with people.' Emphasising the particular significance of being at Cambridge, she added:

> This is the thing, like, being at Cambridge . . . I would never have had the opportunity elsewhere, do you know what I mean, like, contacts? . . . It might sound like really crap but I think it's a really useful skill. I think that's the most important thing about university. It's got nothing to do with your degree. I think it's the resources you pick up and the contacts. My friends are going to go on to, like, important things, and they know how to access things and they know how the system works.

The rather more 'instrumental' tone of this last comment was echoed more strongly by a minority of other students. Robert clearly regarded the social contacts he had established as potentially beneficial for his future career: 'I think from Cambridge people are moving on to positions of influence, and personally I've met a lot of people from playing sport, so that's going to be one of the biggest benefits.'

For most of the students, however, it was the educational effects of this more extended peer interaction that were valued most highly. Many felt that encountering new kinds of people had led them to re-examine the values and assumptions they had been brought up with – not least their political assumptions. Denise contrasted her pre-university existence in rural East Anglia – 'most of my friends' parents and things when I was at school were kind of Conservative' – with the effects of meeting students with a much wider range of political outlooks: 'It has made me think more about where I stand in politics and things; my main change in outlook has been that I *think* more about it.' Many others made similar claims. It was not so much that ultimately their political convictions had been radically changed but that they felt that they now held their views in a more informed and self-critical way. Lydia, for example, said that her experience at university had basically confirmed her previous attitudes but had also made her significantly more reflective:

> I'm probably a lot more political than I was. I always thought the world was a pretty unfair place and now I believe that much more strongly than I did before. At the same time, I've become more open-minded, which is an odd thing to say because both have happened at the same time. But although I believe in things in some ways *more* strongly, I test myself more before I get to a conclusion.

Melanie similarly felt that she had retained her old convictions but was nevertheless more open to taking competing views seriously: 'I think I'm a little less absolute than when I came to university, better at taking on board other people's principles, just better at not responding violently straight away!'

Given that many of the students we interviewed were selected partly because their courses contained a strong social science and/or humanities element, it would be surprising if – at least for some of them – there was not a link between this sort of peer discussion and the content of their courses. Samantha, for example, explained that she had chosen to transfer from Business Studies to Sociology after her first year because of her perception of the different character of students' involvement in these different subject areas:

> I only did Business Studies for one year and that was totally different from doing the Humanities course I'm doing at the moment. With Business Studies, people are more looking for a job ... I mean, although yes, I'm doing it [my present course] because I want to get a job ... But I mainly want to do it because I *enjoy* it ... Doing Sociology and Women's Studies I just want to keep learning.

Laura felt strongly that the content of her course as well as the educative effects of discussion with her peers had both played a major part transforming her into a person who was more socially and politically informed:

Before I came to university I was naïve; I'm ashamed to say how little I knew really, just generally. I just feel now that, you know, I can pick up a newspaper and read it and it makes more sense than it did before.

Nor was it only social science students who felt this way. Abigail described how she had been influenced by the ideas of lecturers in her Biology courses as well as by her peers:

We've been studying conservation ... and you meet quite a lot of lecturers who have quite strong points of view as to what should be going on in politics. So I think they have influenced my point of view ... quite a lot because you've got sort of respect for them ... Friends as well, obviously – living with people who've got different points of view.

Such feelings – of enhanced personal confidence, of being more broadly informed, of having been educated and having educated each other as a result of studying together – were expressed even more strongly by some of the mature students in our group. Tony was typical:

I've come a long way since three years ago in what I know and what I'm confident in talking about. There's so many subjects I wouldn't get involved in – but now I hold my own ... I generally fall into the 'mature student' band and that is because we come from work: we're here for a reason; we know what we're doing and we appreciate being here ... We are just pleased to be doing a degree ... It really does open you up, Sociology as a subject. The teachers, for me, have been fantastic ... and it's that whole learning environment.

As we have already pointed out in Section 4.3, only one of our respondents offered a fully articulated 'classic' justification of higher education in terms of its role in forming an educated citizenry. It is worth at this point returning to Denise's comments and quoting them more fully:

I think we've got ... the obligation as well to inform ourselves about things like politics ... so if you've got the mental capacity to understand it and inform yourself, you should do so ...

because you need a large number of people who really know and really understand these things to kind of, who are going to elect governments, who are going to do the right things, and to push for things ... I think that we've got that kind of responsibility, to be that group of people, you know, not just the middle classes but, you know, that group of people who understand and are intelligent and kind of use it in a constructive way rather than just make themselves money.

While this is certainly a more fully developed rationale than that offered by anyone else in our group, it is worth emphasising that Denise's views are not radically discontinuous with those of many others. And it is also worth stressing that the great majority of the voices we have recorded are clearly in marked contrast to popular images of the current generation of students as simply politically apathetic, hedonistic and self-seeking. Of course, some others in our group *were* significantly less 'engaged' and some freely admitted to remaining uninterested in politics. As Helen put it: 'I don't think my political attitudes have changed at all; I mean, I still don't have much interest', though even she added, 'I don't think I've become more involved but I have become a lot more independent.'

Finally, however, it is significant that even Denise, whose exceptional and articulate plea for graduates to act as the leaders of an educated public we have just cited, nevertheless somewhat shamefacedly confessed to *not* having become at all involved in 'official' politics: 'I still haven't had contact with anybody from a political party, so I've still, you know, no idea how to vote in the General Election or something.' We shall discuss such interesting paradoxes at greater length in the next chapter.

Chapter 5

Citizenship, mutuality and civil society

5.1 Introduction

In the previous chapters we examined and contrasted various models of citizenship and ways in which citizenship is seen as problematic in British society. We also indicated certain issues involved when treating citizenship as a 'problem'. We noted, for instance, that despite the apparent absence of a widely used language of citizenship, Britain in the period after the Second World War nevertheless developed an extensive welfare state that could be seen as embodying and operationalising a strong model of social citizenship. It can also be observed that certain social consequences that could be expected as resulting from a weak sense of citizenship are *not* apparent. In particular, the conduct of everyday life in British society continues, in comparative terms, in a relatively well-ordered and civil way. Admittedly there are periodic outbreaks of soccer hooliganism and rioting and moral panics about muggings and concerns about crime, but as historians have pointed out, such things are themselves part of a long English tradition. However, in terms of indicators such as crime statistics or in the simple experiences of walking the streets, travelling on buses, shopping in high streets, drinking in pubs, life in the public sphere is generally conducted in a safe, courteous and convivial manner for most people in most places most of the time. In these respects, Britain displays what might be termed a high level of *civility* in many aspects of its everyday life.

Given this wider context, it is worth noticing that many of the contemporary worries about citizenship tend to focus upon the relationship between citizens and what one of our interviewees called 'official politics': the instruments and institutions of government and democracy. The low turn-out at the last two UK general elections was one of the factors that precipitated the current run of concerns about the health of citizenship in this country and the 1997 turnout figures were cited in the Crick Report as a justification for introducing citizenship education as a mandatory component of the National Curriculum (Advisory Group on Citizenship 1998). Studies indicating supposed political apathy typically employ indicators such as membership of political parties, the turn-out at elections, knowledge about politicians (e.g. being able to put names and offices to faces), active involvement in the democratic process (e.g. canvassing, helping on election nights). High levels of involvement in selected activities or institutions are taken as healthy signs, and low levels, understandably, as a cause for concern. But does it automatically follow that a low level of involvement implies either apathy and ignorance or else a turning inward towards privatism?

Insofar as the idea of a crisis of citizenship suggests an unwelcome retreat from the social in favour of the self-regarding privatism of the rationally calculating economic individual, it is worth reminding ourselves that what we are talking about here is precisely that entrepreneurial/consumer 'citizen' so enthusiastically promoted by sections of the New Right in the 1980s. And here, we also need to remind ourselves that for thorough-going neo-liberals, it is still the case that markets offer a superior alternative not only to social citizenship but also to those forms of voluntary sector 'active citizenship' so favoured by 'one-nation' Conservatives like Douglas Hurd or Kenneth Baker (see Section 2.3). Were the views of such radical neo-liberals to prevail, there would indeed be a crisis of citizenship, since, from this point of view, it is in many respects *better* to be a consumer than a citizen. However, there appears to be little evidence to support the belief that large numbers of British citizens have been fully won over by this message, despite the energy, even ferocity, of those who promoted it. And as we have seen, it is certainly the case that our interview data show that very few of the students we interviewed came anywhere near to whole-heartedly embracing an identity of this kind. There was, indeed, only one instance of a respondent who clearly saw herself as having, while at university, turned away from what she saw as an 'old Labour' outlook in favour of a more neo-liberal stance:

> When I started university I was ... quite a sympathetic person
> and I was, like, okay, those who are socially disadvantaged,
> you've got to help them and we need, you know, like, 'old
> Labour' policies and philosophy, state intervention, hand-
> outs and that kind of thing. But now it's, like, okay, yes, it
> would be good if there were benefits for people and there
> weren't poor people and disadvantaged people or whatever.
> But life's not like that and you have to ... be responsible ...
> even though, excuse my French, but crap happens, and
> you've got to sort things out for yourself ... No one's going to
> give you stuff or do things for you, so you have to take your
> own responsibility.
>
> (Sara)

Admittedly, a good many more of our respondents had a strong
sense that a further drift towards privatised provision was
somehow inevitable (or at least very probable) but, as we have also
stressed, their feelings about this were at best ambivalent and
most saw it as morally unappealing.

The 'apathy and ignorance' diagnosis of a citizenship crisis is
also questionable. Those who support it are, for the most part,
regretting the unwillingness of many voters, especially young
voters, to get any more than minimally involved in the democratic
process and actively endorse it with their enthusiasm – interpreting this as evidence of a decline in social responsibility and
concern. However, other interpretations are possible. The low
public esteem of politicians is well known and it is generally conceded that aspects of the visible conduct of political life (e.g. as in
the 'ya-boo' politics of televised debates in the House, or spin and
sleaze) contribute to the problem. In another way, an increasingly
presidential style of government and a sense that the Cabinet, let
alone the House of Commons, have little real influence on events
encourage the view there is little point anyway. Insofar as such
analyses are valid, it would follow that the political classes must
put their own house in order as part of any solution to such problems. The point we are making here can be illustrated by considering the possibility of a principled alternative to the actively
assenting citizen. People can withdraw from involvement in the
formal political processes not merely because they do not care but
because, on the contrary, they do. One thing that is being ignored
in much of the mainstream citizenship debate is the possibility of

the actively dissenting citizen who withholds endorsement as a matter of principle because the political processes themselves are not seen as worthy of support. The possibility of such considered and conscientious abstention clearly shows the inadequacy of polarities that simplistically oppose political apathy to a desirable state of active involvement.

It seems to be the case, then, that people can hold a sense of morally ordered social space beyond that of the 'official' political sphere. Our discussion in this chapter will explore an alternative route into this social space, which includes 'citizenship' not through the formal political processes but through certain interpretations of the concepts of *civil society* and *the public sphere*. We will suggest that our respondents' language reveals a strong sense, first, of *sociality* in terms of the quality of engagement with one another, and, second, of *mutuality*, that is, a sense of people being bound by certain relations of mutual reciprocity and influenced by principles of fairness, responsibility, respect and altruism. We will relate these qualities to the 'civic' as opposed to the 'constitutional' aspects of citizenship. Drawing upon historical studies it can be argued that it was the civic model of citizenship that historically was prior and which served as a principle and a resource for criticising and reforming state relations. The sociality and mutuality expressed in our respondents' views are grounded, we suggest, in this civic space and it may be here among other places that we might seek for ways to revitalise the state dimension.

5.2 Studenthood and sociality

In Chapter 4 we examined the ways in which the members of our sample expressed their views concerning the quality of their involvement with other students. As we have said, for many, this was felt to be one of the most valuable aspects of their university experience. It was in this space, for example, that individuals felt that they had most developed as people. Meeting other students from a variety of backgrounds and encountering a wide range of views and experiences and, in particular, observing the varying circumstances among their peers, were the factors most frequently cited as being of significance. As we shall see in Section 5.3, it was the variation in one another's circumstances that led many of them to a sense of unfairness in funding arrangements and made them especially hostile to top-up fees on the grounds that such policies would exacerbate differences and injustice even further. In a common-sense way, what is being indicated here are the social benefits of university life. However, it might be a mistake to rest the analysis there.

In particular, it is worth noting that it was the *exchange of views* that our respondents prized in the social mixture of their student peer group. As was illustrated in Section 4.6, individuals did not necessarily change their own ideas, though many did, but, rather held them with more 'depth', in a more informed way, and often with a greater willingness to listen to others. There is, in this, a personal sense of a developing skill in the handling of ideas and their social exchange. It is important to note that this is not simply an intellectual or academic skill, but a social skill in the management of self and others, and the ideas exchanged are not just those encountered in their courses, but relate just as importantly to personal experiences and points of view. The social space in which students live together as peers structures the distinctive mode of sociality in which these exchanges occur, through conversations in bars and dining halls, in shared student houses or the rooms and landings of college accommodation. In order to get a sense of what our respondents are telling us about their experience in this space, we must project beyond the words contained in the transcripts of their interviews to the daily lives in which these exchanges occurred and appreciate how those exchanges would be regulated by some shared model of civility that made them possible. To be a student, then, is to experience a particular form of sociality within the distinctive space of student life. And, as we argue below, this form of sociality is governed by an invisible but potent code of civil conduct that makes possible the exchanges that our respondents valued so highly and which gives them their quality.

It would be wrong to simplistically assign this crucial aspect of studenthood to the 'informal' side of university life. There are clear continuities between the kinds of values, qualities and skills that are being described by our respondents and the 'formal' procedures of academic life and liberal scholarship. Students during lectures have to develop the discipline of concentrating for a long period of time on the sustained exposition of arguments and positions; they have to become 'patient listeners'. In tutorials they might face the need to explain themselves in more depth or with greater clarity, in seminars they might gain the confidence to speak out in front of others and also learn the etiquette of turn-taking, of treating others with respect and of hearing them out. It is not only in their content that courses of study educate. The disciplines of scholarly discursive practice also instil, because they depend upon, a certain order of rigorous 'civility'. The relevance of this to citizenship is that the 'civil code' of the academy is not only social in *character* (as opposed to the abstract logics of normative epistemology) but is, in a broader sense, social in *origin*, in that it and citizenship developed together in a largely unitary form with the emergence of civil society and the public sphere in the early modern period. Especially in the case of science, crucial early developments actually took place not within the universities (i.e. Oxford and Cambridge) but outside them in the homes of gentleman scientists such as Robert Boyle (Shapin 1994). Most significantly for our argument, in a crucial sense, the development of the public sphere entailed the formalisation of codes of critical enquiry as regulators of conduct in public life, of social relations in civil society. The principle of disinterestedness in the warranting of truth claims in scientific method or in the presentation of literary judgements was historically continuous with the demand for civility in social relations and fairness and justice in the relationship between citizen and state. In the same manner, a common mode of sociality structures the collegiate space of the university from the lecture hall to the landing. And it is no accident that it is precisely this quality that campus and college-type universities proclaim as one of their most distinctive strengths.

5.3 Mutuality

In some of the broader debates about citizenship which we reviewed in the introduction to this chapter, it is sometimes the case that more is seen to be at stake than the mainstream political process itself. The tendency is to associate a withdrawal from the political with a more general tendency to privatism in the sense of a withering away of other kinds of associational networks and modes of involvement in society. A weakening of the political is assumed to imply either a coarsening or an attenuation of the social. However, as we observed above, the quality of everyday life in this country would not necessarily support such an interpretation. It is also the case that our interviewees, as demonstrated in the previous chapter, showed a strong sense of *moral* concern about the quality of relationships. The language of this concern expressed itself in relation to three main circuits of relationships.

The first of these is that to do with *peers* – those who all share the situation of being a student but differ from one another in other respects, most importantly in terms of social origins that are associated with advantage or disadvantage within the student condition. Here, the major principle was that of *fairness*. In their everyday interactions with one another, and as an aspect of the social learning experiences we have discussed in Section 5.2, our respondents found themselves involved in the management of similarity and difference in the social relations of student life. It was a certain kind of difference that was most welcomed: the differences of background and experience. However, other kinds of differences were judged to be pernicious and unfair. Implicit in such judgements is a sense of equality in some fundamental respect. Our respondents' sense of injustice is tied to a moral sense of the kinds of differences that difference should make, and a tacit sense that a measure of equity be preserved in certain key respects despite differences elsewhere. It is striking that this principle is affirmed even when respondents recognise that they themselves would not be disadvantaged by, indeed might even gain from, arrangements such as top-up fees. In a general sense, our sample – at least in these respects – represented the principle that fairness and social justice are worthwhile in their own right and are conditions that individuals would be willing to make some sacrifice for. From individual to individual, these ideas were expressed with varying degrees of explicitness and strength, but, certainly the language they spoke was much more that of mutuality than of privatised calculation.

The second circuit is the *intergenerational* one defined by family. In this case the principle invoked is that of altruistic reciprocity. These students are very aware of what their parents (or sometimes their partners and other relatives) have contributed to their being at university. The moral sense here is complex and resonates with what Crouch picks out by his term 'community' (Crouch 2001 and see Section 3.2). In the first place it is understood in terms of what parents should do for children (carrying the implication that they will do likewise for theirs) and that this is done with no expectation of a return. On a number of occasions, the term 'investment' was used, but then immediately separated from investment in an economic calculative sense: the parents do not expect anything back in return. At the same time, interviewees typically say that they will look after their parents in old age, but not as a quid pro quo or even because it is 'expected' of them, but as an act of reciprocal altruism, or goodness for its own sake. It is important to understand that what is being referred to is not just the student's particular family (kith and kin) but – at least in some measure – a principle governing families or intergenerational relations in general. The sense of unfairness noted in relation to the peer circuit was often rooted in the differential effects of policy, given other students' differing family circumstances.

The third circuit is that of the relationship with the *state*. This is far from explicit in the sense that interviewees rarely talk about 'the state' and only slightly more often mention 'the government', etc. Rather, these institutions are implied by the way in which our respondents see student loans as responsible for unfairness in the other two areas. Loans place inequitable and unfair burdens upon some students from other countries or from certain social backgrounds. At the same time, parents have been unduly burdened in supporting their children through university and called upon to give up too much (holidays, etc.) in order to do so. In many cases, it was, as we have seen (Section 4.6), the fact of being in the firing line of government policy that sensitised our respondents to the social impact of policy and to some degree 'politicised' their attitudes. This was not so simply because of how policy affected them personally, but also because of their awareness of how it affected others.

Implicit within the moralism of the language of these three circuits is a complex underlying sense of a proper ordering of relationships and of the principles that govern them. There is a shared sense among our sample that this order has not been maintained within the circuits of student peers and family: there is too much difference between peers who should be in key respects similar, and too much is (opportunistically?) demanded by government of the spontaneous reciprocal altruism between parents and children. This sense of a fair ordering of social relationships is also apparent in the answers to various questions concerning state welfare and benefits, and their recipients (Section 4.3). In this case, the concern is with a fourth circuit of '*abstract others*' (people suffering but also fulfilling certain conditions) who are not 'real' to our interviewees in the way that their fellow students and parents are real, but who nevertheless constitute a sympathetically imagined community beyond the self and towards which certain responsibilities are assumed – albeit conditionally.

Hence, although the majority of our respondents are typical in exhibiting the lack of interest in, knowledge of and even confusion about the formal political process, it would not be correct to see them also as having withdrawn into privatism and an associated personal calculativeness. In the first instance, they clearly locate themselves with others within a variety of wider social spaces. In the second case, these spaces are not merely contexts of shared communication but are also moral spaces, structured by principles of fairness and equity, altruism and reciprocity. In the case of the 'global missionaries' considered earlier, these principles are extended within a global space and the sense of responsibility to others goes far beyond family or nation. Although, as our categories indicate, our sample could be divided into groups that by some criteria differed radically, in respect to the things being considered here, there was also a remarkable sense of unanimity. Those who were intending to cash in their qualifications for the highest market value are not distinguished from the global missionaries or those going into national public service by a radically different fundamental value-set in these terms. Rather, their language reveals an attempt to reconcile their choice with a concern with a moral sense of social order – if only through the idea that as high-earners they will also be high tax-payers – that does not differ fundamentally from that of their fellows.

In a contingent historical sense, our sample is, by accident of birth, a sample of 'Thatcher's children' and the climate in which they become students was one that included a partial privatisation of the costs of higher education. If, on the one hand, university education is perceived as a personal investment, does, on the other, a degree come to be seen as simply a commodity to be cashed in for the highest return? As far as our sample is concerned, the answer, as we have seen, is very much, no. Although, certainly, some of our respondents did acknowledge instrumentalism among sections of the student body (e.g. the young woman referred to in Section 4.6 who switched from Business Studies to Sociology), in the main our respondents did not speak a language of educational commodification. For many, the prime purpose of education remained vocational in relation to employment in the public services, and for others, especially the mature students, it was primarily a life-enhancing experience. Their perceptions of social space were strongly structured by a sense of *moral* economy where relations are governed by principles rather than reduced to 'the cash nexus'. Unlike Mrs Thatcher, they do not believe that there is 'no such thing as society'. But what is most significant, from our point of view, is that 'society' is not present simply as an abstract concept but substantiated in terms of distinct social spaces identified in the circuits we described above and instantiated in the relations lived out in those spaces: in relations, especially, with fellow students and between generations, with boundaries that are not merely local and immediate, but extending to collectivities of generation, the disadvantaged, the nation and beyond. It is in this intermediate dimension of the social, between the local and the general (what in sociological terms might be termed the Durkheimian level of the social), that we believe we can recover from our respondents' talk the traces of citizenship.

In sum, our purpose in the analysis above has not been, in the more conventional manner, to formally summarise the values and opinions expressed by our respondents in their interviews. Rather, it has sought to explicate their sense of the social by identifying the spaces in which they live their lives, how those spaces are structured according to certain principles, and how life in those spaces is regulated by particular codes of sociality. In their speech, our respondents recognised four circuits: (i) those of student peers; (ii) the intergenerational; (iii) that of imagined 'abstracts others' as recipients of state welfare; (iv) and the formal constitutional dimension of their relationship to state and government. These circuits were governed by principles such as fairness, altruism, reciprocity and responsibility that we will sum up in the more general term, 'mutuality'. Their language gives insight into a complex sense of the social as a structured moral economy that links the local and immediate with the general and abstract. The moralising of extended relationships in this manner counters both the fears of those who believe that the absence of a language of formal citizenship indicates privatised withdrawal and those who would wish to celebrate the primacy of calculative individualism. This sense of the social, we contend, reveals certain significant traces and sediments of citizenship and we will now broaden the analysis by relating these points to a more general and primarily historical discussion of civil society and the public sphere.

5.4 Forms of citizenship involvement: being 'civic' without being 'political'

As we have argued, the conventional view that posits the current situation of perceived political apathy as a fundamental problem, is that citizenship is centrally to do with the active involvement of the individual in the formal processes of democratic government. However, in its formative period the early phases of the emergence of citizenship arguably had at least as much to do with keeping government at bay or at arm's length as with involving the individual with it. Citizenship developed not, in the first instance, in the relationship between the generality of citizens and the state, but in the relationship between citizen and citizen, and those relationships were lived out not in the polis, but in the structuring of civil society within what gradually became recognised as the public sphere. It was here that the principle was displayed that provided the basis for critique of government and a measure of its shortcomings. Citizenship has its origins in the public sphere as a normative principle that provided a critical test for the way in which government treated people.

It is not our intention when employing the term 'public sphere', here, to engage in detail with the ideas of Jürgen Habermas. Since his seminal work (first published in English as recently as 1989), numerous others have taken up the idea for a variety of purposes (see Blanning 2002, Introduction) and, in what follows, we will be drawing upon a number of such writers. Our interest in the concept of the public sphere is to establish a substantive link between citizenship and the qualities of sociality and mutuality we have described above. In this respect, our main concern is with the manner in which our respondents spontaneously represent 'social space' as structured in terms of distinct circuits of relations regulated by moral principles that govern the relationships between people. It is certainly the case that the *discursive* qualities of student sociality that we discussed are close to Habermas' focus upon the dialogic features of the late eighteenth-century bourgeois public sphere, but we do not intend to follow this any further into the complexities of his theory of communicative action, let alone those associated with modern communication technology and the idea of a 'refeudalisation' of the public sphere (Thompson 1994). Our primary concern is to demonstrate the underlying continuities between mutuality and citizenship and the discontinuities between mutuality and certain aspects of the contemporary political processes.

What can be discerned in the language of our sample is, perhaps, symptomatic of something that is deeply rooted in the history of citizenship; in Lindsay Paterson's words, 'a tension between two versions of public:civic or state' (2000: 39). In the first chapter of this book, we contrasted the weak language of citizenship in Britain with David Cannandine's historical examination of the strong language of class (Cannadine 1998). In a parallel fashion, some historical reflections might also open the way to exploring an alternative 'civic' language (or sensibility) of citizenship that may retain a vitality that is lacking in the 'state' language and may suggest also why the latter has become so relatively enfeebled. The theme of Paterson's essay is close to our own concerns, 'Civil Society and Democratic Renewal'. His case is that of Scotland and the problem raised by a 'society without a state' after the parliament was removed to London after the Act of Union. It is worth following Paterson's argument in some detail. On the one hand, he considers society without a state as a problem for Scottish philosophers in the eighteenth century but, on the other, he also discusses the ways in which networks of social capital sustained the distinctive fabric of Scottish sociality and solidarity through into the twentieth century when, in the 1980s, the profound distaste for Thatcherism ruling from south of the border fuelled support for devolution and a new Scottish Parliament.

In the case of the Scottish philosophers, Paterson cites those major Enlightenment thinkers such as Hume and Ferguson and, later, Adam Smith whose concern was with the manner in which the members of a society maintain a sense of the social in terms of a common mutuality that was 'at once, anti-statist and yet public, private and yet moral, depoliticised – in one sense of politics – and yet civic' (ibid.: 43). Under the peculiar conditions that prevailed in Scotland, Paterson argues, this sense continued to constitute a 'highly moral public sphere'. Substantively, this public sphere was constituted through networks of citizens (especially professional groups) that serviced and sustained society not through the political processes of the state but those of civil society. In Paterson's words, 'Civil society is autonomous, and the networks of social capital which it embodies are first of all the autonomous activities of citizens, not the state' (ibid.: 52). Crucially, the point here is that it is 'possible to be sceptical about the state and yet not private' (ibid.: 51). We must be clear, at this point, that it is not our intention to be in principle anti-statist: that is not the purpose of the argument. (And in this respect it is significant that Paterson's analysis applies to an exceptional historical situation in which the state had removed itself.) It is also important to stress that Paterson's reading of Adam Smith does not endorse the possessive-individualist simplifications of Thatcherite neo-liberalism; indeed, it holds those who make Smith the patron saint of neo-liberalism as being deeply in error. Rather, the issue is the way in which the Scottish case, for all its historical particularity, still throws into relief those spaces in which individuals can feel themselves 'citizens' without having involvement in formal political processes. In much the same way that people can feel themselves to be religious without being members of a church, so they can feel themselves 'civic' without being 'political' in the narrow sense (which is not to say that civil society does not have a politics of its own, as Paterson illustrates). A distancing from the 'narrowly' political can, as we have suggested earlier, take a number of forms: principled dissent, generalised scepticism, a sense that the personal involvement in the political process lacks efficacy – as well as the state of uniformed apathy more commonly depicted. But, with the exception of the last of these, the others are in a sense and to differing degrees 'principled', in that the state relationship is judged as wanting relative to the moral ordering of other spheres of the social in civil society.

In his concluding general discussion of 'social capital', Paterson makes a final point of some significance:

> It [social capital] describes structures, not content ... It is analogous to the distinction drawn by theorists of civil society between its institutions as a morally neutral network of exchange and their role as a morally respectable bulwark against amoral state power and amoral free markets ... The moral conclusions drawn from civic networks by late-twentieth century feminists, say, might be quite different from those drawn by mid-nineteenth century bourgeois men, but the role of social networks in making morality practical is common.
>
> (ibid.: 54)

The distinction made here between structures and content, on the one hand, and the process of 'making morality practical', on the other, are key ideas. As far as the latter is concerned, it is at least something akin to this that we can sense in the language of our interviewees when they are talking about the various circuits of relationships within which they feel themselves to be located and their moral economies. Clearly, our respondents wish to see themselves as moral beings. None adopts a language of calculative privatism. Their morality is made practical (and is practised) within networks or spaces that are essentially civil in character and one way in which this occurs is in that process of mutual political learning that was so central to our respondents' appreciation of the student experience. In the case of the former – structures and content – the point has to do with Habermas' classic formulation of 'the public sphere' and also with some of the standard criticisms of that formulation, and we will return to these later.

5.5 Mutuality and the public sphere

As Habermas described it in his seminal study, the public sphere emerged in the latter part of the eighteenth century as that space in which citizens came together to exchange and formulate ideas. There are two crucial components to this situation: the first is to do with what was debated and the second to do with how. As far as the 'what' is concerned, it was society itself. As James Chandler (1998) demonstrates, during the eighteenth century a new literature begins to appear concerned specifically to describe 'the state' of the nation (a genre of the state). In particular, this literature assumed the form of annual registers of events (ibid.: Chapter 2). The critical focus of these observations was the state itself – the state of the state, as it were. (The critical relationship between the different senses of the same word was captured towards the end of the twentieth century in the title of Will Hutton's (1995) book *The State We're In*). More broadly, what is being displayed here is that deepening of reflexivity in modernity in which society itself becomes a visible object of analysis and critique. Government comes to be held accountable for the 'state of the nation' and it is in this situation, Habermas argued, that 'public opinion' comes into being as a force in its own right. Chandler describes how:

The 'public sphere' that formed the object of Shelley's and Hunt's private correspondence about the 'state England is in' in the closing days of 1819 was thus deeply and habitually structured by the annualised representation of society, politics, and culture. When he asked Hunt to match his sonnet with a 'paper ... on the actual state of the country' on the eve of the last week of 1819, Shelley would have been mobilising the resources of that domain. Moreover ... he may also have been recalling Hunt's bold prediction from the first week of the year, that 1819 would be 'one of the most important years that have been seen for a long while ... [for] a spirit is abroad'.

(1998: 124–5)

Chandler draws attention to the complex interactions between a number of things: as already mentioned, the manner in which society becomes differentiated as an object, how it has a 'condition' or 'state' that is open to description and judgement, how these states become periodised and subject to review through time (in a 'periodical' press) in terms of whether things are better or worse, and how government is held to be responsible and accountable. To employ Chandler's words, 'In relating the State to "the state" and its transformations' (ibid.: 126), it is 'the spirit of the age' that is being sought for: that to which Shelley is giving expression in his sonnet 'England' in 1819 ('An old, mad, blind, despised and dying king: Princes, the dregs of their dull race, who flow through public scorn ...') and that he requested Hunt to convey in a different way in the paper he requests from him. Chandler says that the *Oxford English Dictionary* cites Shelley's use of the phrase, 'spirit of the age' in 1820 as the first recorded usage – though Chandler himself has earlier examples. It is in the mobilisation of the 'resources' of the domain of the public sphere (especially of 'public scorn') that the connection is made between the 'what' and the 'how'. The public sphere being described, here, is that of principled and reasoned dissent from arbitrary or absolutist, non-representative government.

What is at stake, here, is effectively displayed by David Norbrook (1999). Norbrook's concern is with the English Republic and he extends the historical time frame of the public sphere back into the seventeenth century:

With the collapse of censorship in England in the 1640s, the political debates that were at first conducted obliquely through the dramatisation and publication of the classics became more urgent and direct. This period arguably saw the first appearance of what Jürgen Habermas has termed the 'bourgeois public sphere'. This he defines as a space for the critical discussion of public issues independent of the traditional monopolies of discourse held by the church, the court, and the professions. This was 'bourgeois' in the Marxist sense of belonging to an emergent middle class; but Habermas is concerned with the bourgeois not merely as homo economicus but as citizen, as exercising positive public responsibility as well as a negative freedom from old economic and social ties. Habermas' model has been criticised as idealising and schematic . . . Yet his model is helpful, not least because of the congruence between its own terms and those of seventeenth century republicans. Habermas' development of speech-act theory can be seen as one more attempt at recovering the spirit of the classical forum and adapting it to modern conditions.

(ibid.: 13)

The key term in Norbrook's statement is the view of the 'citizen' as 'exercising positive public responsibility'. The contrast we have made earlier between the neo-liberal and the 'social' models of citizenship first assumes something that is recognisable as akin to its modern form in the seventeenth century, in the distinction between that (Hobbesian) calculative model of the person that MacPherson (1964) refers to as 'possessive individualism' and the liberal (or 'social') *citizen* where individualism is defined not in opposition to the social but in and through it. It is this principle that constitutes civil society as the primary domain of citizenship. It is the relationship between citizens in that space that constructs the paradigm for the constitutional link between citizens and representative government. The language of citizenship is both constitutional (citizen and government – a 'vertical' relationship) and also (horizontally) about relationships in civil society: a language of what, in a particular sense, can be termed 'civility'. This expresses in a different way Paterson's 'tension' between the civic and the state. And as expressed, for instance, in the debates of an even earlier period over the franchise in the New Model Army, the constitutional issue was, as much as anything, a debate about civility – about the relationships between those who were joined in a common struggle but still divided by social rank and economic interest (MacPherson 1964; Shapin 1994).

Jonathan Israel, in his study of 'Radical Enlightenment' (2001) has pointed out that:

> Historians in recent decades have become conscious of the evolution in western and central Europe during the century and a half before the French Revolution of a wholly new kind of public sphere for debate, exchange of ideas, and opinion forming, located outside the formal consultative procedures and assemblies of the past, a public sphere which emerged only where a high degree of social and cultural interchange existed outside the deliberations of formal political, judicial, and ecclesiastical bodies and institutions. Among the novelties in European life in generating this forum of public opinion formation beyond the sway of princely courts, the judiciary, the Church, and Parliament were the new erudite journals, universal libraries, literary clubs, lexicons, and encyclopaedias ... as well as, more mundanely, newspapers, gentleman's magazines, tea- and coffee-houses and, after around 1730, also Masonic Lodges.
>
> (ibid.: 59)

It is within this 'wholly new kind of public sphere' that the modern citizen emerges and it is in terms of the transformations of the public sphere that changing modes of citizenship need to be located. In the passage above, Israel stresses the separation between the public sphere and 'the sway of princely courts', etc.: the formal organs of pre-democratic government. He also mentions, and in his study describes in detail, the European-wide dimension of the public sphere of philosophers, intellectuals and scholars: Gibbon's 'Great Republic'. A similar point could be made with regard to scientific experimentalists in the same period and those two groups, of course, were not as sharply distinguished then as they are today (Shapin 1994). The emergence of the citizen was enacted through new codes of personal conduct in everyday life and they were intrinsically entwined with an emerging model of liberal, critical scholarship.

Roy Porter quotes Voltaire's comment on the Royal Exchange

in London: 'There the Jew, the Mahometan, and the Christian transact together as tho' they all profess'd the same religion, and give the name of Infidel to none but bankrupts' (2000: 21). The 'philosophe', Porter says, is 'depicting men content – differing, but agreeing to differ' (ibid.). Porter sees the more general state that he illustrates here, as indicative of a 'new praxis of personal and social adjustment':

> The accent on refinement was no footling obsession with petty punctilio; it was a desperate remedy meant to heal the chronic social conflict and personal traumas stemming from civil and domestic tyranny and topsey-turvy social values. Politeness could be taught by education … Above all, the refinement of the self was to be a function of energetic sociability … Clubs like Mr. Spectator's, masonic lodges, taverns, coffee houses and friendly societies – miniature free republics of rational society – sprang up to promote fellowship and good feeling.
>
> (ibid.: 22)

The formation of the public sphere brought forth new modes of sociality, new codes of conduct and sociability. Citizens were defined not just by their relationship to the state but by their relationship to each other and it was in terms of that yardstick of civility that the relationship of the state to the people was judged. Civility directs attention to another dimension of the discourse of citizenship, that concerned with how people see their relationships with others rather than with political institutions.

Our suspicion is that at least some of the most highly publicised aspects of the debate about citizenship in modern Britain has been too much preoccupied with the (vertical) constitutional relationship between citizen and state to the neglect of the (horizontal) dimension of relationships in the public sphere, the relationship of civility. In Paterson's view, the Scottish case illustrates, 'a public sphere that was prior to the state, and from which the state derived its authority' (2000: 46). While acknowledging the seminal contribution of Habermas, the writers we have mentioned above push back the emergence of the public sphere to earlier dates: for Norbrook it was a vital principle of English republicanism in the Civil War period. Taken together, these studies expand the scope of the public sphere in both time and

space, but share with each other and with Habermas the view that
its distinctive mode of sociality was discursive, essentially to do
with the way in which people spoke together and the code that
regulated that speech, a code that combined rationality with
sociability, civility with critique in the social mediation of similarity and difference. This aspect of Habermas' analysis has been
stressed by John Thompson (1994) in relation to the significance
of print and the press in the broader argument:

> His way of thinking about print was based on a model of com-
> munication based on the spoken word: the periodical press
> was part of a conversation begun and continued in the shared
> locales of bourgeois sociability. The press was interwoven so
> closely with the life of the clubs and coffee-houses that it was
> inseparable from it ... In this respect, Habermas' account of
> the bourgeois public sphere bears the imprint of the classical
> Greek conception of public life: the salons, clubs and coffee-
> houses of Paris and London were the equivalent, in the
> context of early modern Europe, of the assemblies and mar-
> ketplaces of Ancient Greece. As in Ancient Greece, so too in
> early modern Europe, the public sphere was constituted
> above all in speech, in the weighing up of different argu-
> ments, opinions and points of view in the dialogical exchange
> of spoken words in a shared locale.
>
> (ibid.: 97)

It is this that is echoed in the sense of mutuality expressed by our
respondents and which is lived through in the process of mutual
political learning. The key issue, today, is the relationship
between that space and the formal political discourses of the constitutional dimension of citizenship.

5.6 The structure of civil society

This returns us to the discussion of Paterson's point about the
separation between structure and content in civil society. To a
considerable extent, educational initiatives in citizenship education tend to focus upon content, especially in attempting to install
in pupils the idea of political involvement as an imperative: something that they should do, a responsibility that they should shoul-
der. Beneath the surface lurks the assumption, also informing

other areas such as health, sex and drugs education, that certain types of undesirable behaviour reflect simply ignorance and apathy – 'if only these people knew better they would see how they should behave'. But it might be that it is the structure rather than the content that is the key issue.

Paterson's distinction between content and structure can be related to the standard criticisms that have been raised about Habermas' original account of the late eighteenth-century public sphere. The first (essentially that implied by Paterson) has to do with its male and bourgeois character. The second is to do with the separation of the public and the private – more specifically, this concerns the literary character of the coffee-houses and the relative neglect of science, experimental method and the laboratory 'housed' in the homes of gentleman scientists. As far as the first is concerned, the point is that the standard criticism of Habermas (summarised in Thompson (1994)) is that he fails to acknowledge the particular class and gendered character of the public sphere he describes. Those who do acknowledge its exclusionary features point to the existence of alternative or parallel plebeian (e.g. in corresponding societies) or female spheres (e.g. in the salons). In this form, the picture suggested is of a number of spheres, each relatively homogenous and specialised to particular membership groups. It is this that Paterson appears to be contesting. An extended treatment of this point can be found (independently) in Blanning's (2002) *The Culture of Power and the Power of Culture*. The essential point is made as follows:

> the public sphere that emerged in the course of the eighteenth century cannot be described as 'bourgeois' in a social sense, given the high proportion of clergymen and nobles of various types who operated within it. Socially, the public sphere was more like Noah's Ark than a merchantman. All those who wished to flourish in this new metaphorical space had to come to terms with its essentially meritocratic nature.
>
> (ibid.: 12)

The New Model Army was also more 'ark than merchantman' in its social composition and also in the range of positions (including constitutional monarchists) within it. So, also, is the modern mass university. If Blanning's perspective is adopted (and Porter would seem to be suggesting something similar), then the public sphere is not only further extended in time than Habermas suggests, but also in social space. Its structure is complex: from the coffee-houses, to the salons, to the laboratories in which people gathered to witness (and bear testimony to) experiments conducted according to methods that were by their nature 'meritocratic' in Blanning's sense. Within this extended space, people of different social ranks and, in some cases, of both sexes gathered to exchange ideas according to criteria that required the disregarding of ascribed differences. In this respect, science is, perhaps, more instructive than the literary culture of the coffee-houses. Skilled artisans played a crucial role not only as instrument designers, but as acknowledged experimentalists (Shapin 1994), and as late as the nineteenth century female scientists such as Ada Lovelace could still only demonstrate behind the closed doors of the home experiments that they could not perform publicly (Wooley 1999).

Hence, the relationship between public and domestic spaces, between social rank and gender was not, perhaps, as straightforward as either Habermas' original restricted formulation or the standard criticisms suggest. As Paterson indicates and Blanning more fully argues, what may be truly significant about the emergence of the public sphere, the formation of civil society, was less its content than its structure. In a more sharply political sense, much the same point could be made for the latter part of the eighteenth century for the radical circle within that space of figures such as Tom Paine (Keane 1995), William Godwin and Mary Wollstonecraft – and a generation later, Shelley, Byron and Mary Wollstonecraft/Godwin (Mary Shelley) (Foot 1984). Blanning indicates the complexity of the classic public sphere when he says that:

> Just as the public sphere was socially heterogeneous, so it was politically multi-directional. It was not an agenda but a space in which all kinds of opinions could be expressed, including those which were supportive of the status quo.
>
> (2002: 12)

The distinction here between 'agenda' and 'space' parallels Paterson's between 'content' and 'structure'. For our purposes, Blanning provides a crucial formulation:

While the feudal public sphere had been founded on authority, received passively, the essence of the bourgeois public
sphere is rational argument. The bourgeois public sphere can
be defined as the medium through which private persons can
reason in public. In doing so, they perform the vital function
of mediating relations between the essentially separate realms
of civil society and the state ... What matters about it is not
what it contains in terms of ideas or feelings or even its social
composition, but the fact that those concerns are actively
communicated. It is the effort of communication which
creates the 'public' and gives it qualities of cohesion and
authority quite different from mere aggregates of individuals.

(ibid.: 8–9)

If we understand 'private persons' to entail those specificities of
difference that were so crucial to our students, then Blanning's
formula of 'private persons reasoning in public' well encapsulates
the sociality of student life. What Paterson terms 'making morality
practical' is achieved through Blanning's 'effort of communication', and it is this that we can discern within our interviewees'
desire to retain a sense of themselves as moral actors, and it is a
sense of a civil society beyond the narrowly political that provides
the space in which that desire can be lived out.

These more recent uses of the concept of public sphere differ
from both Habermas' own and some of the earlier critiques in the
following respects:

First, they extend the concept in time and space. For Norbrook
its shape can be discerned within the conflicts of the English
Republic and in the crucial debates within the New Model Army
concerning the franchise. The same issues (at root the problem of
disinterested judgement) are involved in the social problem of
warranting truth claims in experimental method (Shapin 1994)
and these concerns were lodged within enlightened European
networks of thinkers engaged internationally in the effort of communication in 'The Great Republic'.

Second, they extend its complexity. Earlier critics pointed to
Habermas' narrowly bourgeois and masculinist conception of the
public sphere and pointed to the existence of plebeian and
female alternatives. However, these approaches tend to posit
spaces that are to a high degree homogenous and hermetically
sealed from each other and where a specific identity (bourgeois,

male, plebeian, etc.) is the constitutive principle. This type of focus upon content or agenda generally follows from the socially reductive character of analyses through various kinds of standpoint or interest-theoretic perspectives in which structure and procedure are collapsed into content. The more recent studies we have referred to instead present a public sphere that is heterogeneous, multipolitical and where barriers are permeable rather than exclusionary, relatively open rather than emphatically standpoint-relative, and incommensurable.

Third, they call into question a too simplistic division between the public sphere and the domestic as well as the gendering of that division. Although the coffee-house culture described by Habermas was in an obvious sense in 'public places', in significant instances the public sphere extended into the domestic spaces of the home, not only in the form of upper-class female salons but also in the laboratories of gentlemen scientists. At the same time, with regard to the literary character of the public coffee-houses, it can be noted that many literary critics and historians today stress the predominantly feminised character of both readership and authorship in eighteenth-century England. Positionings within the public sphere are more interesting in their anomalous rather than in their dichotomous character. This is important for us because much of the sociality of student life that we have described and that is so important to our students, takes place in the 'private' places of student accommodation and sociability. The public sphere should be understood in terms of structures and principles rather than in terms of places and agendas.

Finally, by virtue of the above, this model of the public sphere emphasises the civil mediation of difference rather than the imposition of limited, exclusionary and self-interested agendas. It requires of all involved an effort of communication – essentially, to learn to listen to others. Against the reductionism of standpoint and interest-theoretic approaches, it recovers a principle of autonomy for the public sphere that leads back to those notions of universalism that are central to the modern concept of the citizen, but does so not through principles of abstract reasoning, but through an examination of substantive modes of sociality and their civil codes.

As far as citizenship, democracy and education are concerned, the crucial link is that between codes of social civility and modes of critical inquiry. Today it is within the university that the latter are still primarily lodged (though we noted that in the seventeenth and eighteenth centuries this was not necessarily the case and contemporary observers such as Delanty (2000) note that the university is possibly losing its monopoly on the production of knowledge) and in a mass higher education system it may provide the platform for a model of sociality in which students can experience mutual political learning in a potentially formative way. However, in terms of full and effective citizenship, this experience must be more than simply one of sociability. In the Civil War period and its aftermath, in the decades between 1780 and 1820 or in 1848 and 1967–8 the sociality of civil society and its sense of mutuality were the critical force in a drive for social reform far removed from the 'footling obsession with petty punctilio' which Porter derides. And the sociality and sense of mutuality revealed by our students were also much more than 'mere' civility in that trivial manner to which Porter here alludes. On the contrary, their moral sense was highly charged within the circuits we described. The problem, rather, is in the *relationship* between the discourses of civic and state citizenship. Rather than apathetic, their relationship to the formal political dimension of citizenship might be better described as one of attenuation. It is not that they do not care, but that there is, for them, little sense of the political process as an effective mechanism through which that caring (or potentiality for caring) can be expressed or meaningfully realised. What is lacking, perhaps, is a political discourse that can reconnect our students' sense of mutuality with issues and state citizenship in the energised and urgent way that characterised the public sphere in earlier times.

5.7 Conclusion

Our purpose in presenting this historical review of the relationship between citizenship and civil society has been to suggest that that quality of 'mutuality' that we discern within our respondents' replies can be related to something that is substantial and formative in the history of citizenship itself. In this sense, the 'problem' of citizenship can be posed in a rather different way. It is not so much that of 'absence' as of a disjunction or discontinuity between various aspects of citizenship in the fullest sense: an attenuated relationship between the civic and the state dimensions. In these terms, it is important for us to stress at this point that we are *not* positing the civic public as an *alternative* to the state (that social capital absolves the state from social responsibility or from taking a leading role in investing economic capital in social services) as might some kinds of communitarianism or advocates of voluntary association and action. While acknowledging the *historical* priority of civil society in the formation of modern citizenship, we fully recognise that its key contribution was the critical transformation of government and the state relationship – the two are entwined and the state is now indispensable to the protection and promotion of social citizenship. However, this also suggests that citizenship education and the promotion of active citizenship do not guarantee more enthusiastic active assenters – they could equally (insofar as its content and pedagogy sought to promote rational autonomy) produce active, principled *dissent*. The basis for this might well be a 'praxis of personal and social adjustment', in Porter's words, rather than a clearly identifiable content or subject matter (which is not to imply that there are not perfectly good reasons to teach such a subject matter anyway). This idea of a 'praxis' or form of sociality is expressed by each of those writers we referred to above in their own particular ways: as 'making morality practical', as the 'effort of communication', and so on, and it is these qualities which we associate with our respondents' sense of mutuality.

In the first chapter of this book we referred to citizenship as an invisible phenomenon with strong effects. This discussion of mutuality and the public sphere makes possible an alternative perspective through which certain important attributes of citizenship do become visible (though still not expressed in a *language* of citizenship), and in terms of which certain of these strong effects can be explained. From this point of view, what is important is that our respondents do have a complex sense of society, that their attitude towards it is morally charged and that, especially in the university, these things are 'made practical' through a substantive mode of sociality in student life. It is the tendency for that effort to fall short of significant engagement with the formally political that constitutes one of the key problems of citizenship in modern Britain: fewer than 20 per cent of first-time voters in the 1997 General Election actually voted (*The Guardian*, 10 April 2002).

Chapter 6

Conclusion
Concerns, hopes and fears

6.1 Introduction

It is unlikely that three academic authors in search of an invisible phenomenon, and faced with the thoughts of thirty students, will come to precisely the same conclusions. These final comments are an attempt to identify the range of reactions, both to what has been said in the interviews and to the debates surrounding the issue of higher education and citizenship. While our concerns are shared, we have not always agreed completely on the significance for the future of the sentiments expressed by the students.

6.2 Concerns

This book began its life with a set of concerns arising from two apparently unconnected educational policies developed in the first years of the New Labour government. These were, first, the loss of a citizen's right (for those appropriately qualified) to free higher education and, second, the institution of citizenship education as a mandatory element of the National Curriculum in England. Our suspicion was that because the policies of loans and fees for higher education seemed to be built upon earlier initiatives promoting privatisation and the enterprising individual, introducing citizenship education into the National Curriculum might be little more than a convenient way of adding a social gloss to an educational system which, in many ways, was increasingly devoted to individual instrumentalism.

Consequently, in Part I, we looked at both the citizenship debates which informed discussions about citizenship education, and at some of the institutional changes in and around higher education which could be seen as potentially challenging to the notion of social citizenship which we espoused. In Part II, students' talk about their university experiences and their future plans for work and private life was analysed for possible signs of emerging new forms of citizenship (such as commitment to neo-liberal 'citizenship') and also for evidence of continuities with the past. The concept of 'Thatcher's children' was used by one of our respondents who, being active in student politics, bemoaned the fact that many of his fellow students seemed to be interested only in obtaining a degree good enough to secure them a well-paid job. As he put it, 'Everyone is here to get the best job, to get the best degree and the most money'. The implication was that they cared little for others, and even less for the social and political issues of the day.

Now it is undeniable that many of the students we interviewed were children during the years of successive Thatcher administrations and lived in families which felt the effects of her policies. And it may well be that it was there – in the private worlds of family and household – where their own reactions to politics, and their philosophies of life, may have been mainly formed. Yet, as our evidence clearly shows, in the majority of cases, they did *not* end up as 'Thatcher's children' in spirit. And one main reason for this was that those policies with which she was associated had such different and unequal private effects – even within the middle classes from which most of our interviewees were drawn. It may indeed have been the case that those policies encouraged people to look out for themselves and their families, to concentrate on 'me and mine', and 'putting the family first' – as the titles of various social commentaries suggested at the time. However, some of those families were systematically advantaged by the policies while others suffered from their effects. Throughout these interviews, we found echoes from the experience of families which had gained and also from those which had lost (for example in Section 4.5). For these reasons, it is difficult for most of these students to see themselves as 'Thatcher's children', because, unlike Christians, citizens cannot be simply 'born again'. For good or bad, the conditions *for* citizenship and consciousness *of* citizenship may change, but citizens themselves are embedded in the continuities of both private lives and public institutions, and it is some of these continuities which may be seen as giving hope to those who believe that social citizenship has contemporary relevance and is worth trying to sustain.

6.3 Hopes

For those who may subscribe to the view of social citizenship represented in this book some measure of comfort can be found in the responses of the small group of students we interviewed. Many do have an awareness of national boundedness and they retain some sense of still belonging to a community of fate. Furthermore, their reactions indicate that they can be regarded as socially concerned citizens in many ways – even if many feel distanced from conventional forms of political involvement. It was quite clear that few saw themselves as individualised consumers and investors in higher education. Furthermore, the universities they were attending continued to act, for them at least, as open public institutions.

What was evident was that our respondents had a sense of belonging to a society of structured social spaces which they still saw as regulated by moral principles. They spoke a language of what we termed 'mutuality', which involved reciprocity in their relations with one another and a consciousness of fairness and justice. It would, of course, be unreal to imagine that the university developed these qualities in the first place. Rather, the students had a strong sense that these were the qualities that had been most *developed* and refined by the student experience. The most significant feature of this process was the sociality of student life, especially meeting people from different backgrounds and exchanging experiences, values and views. The sociality they described in the social spaces of student life was one governed by a code of civility in relationships with others and we noted that this was, in certain respects, continuous with the formal procedures and codes of academic life and scholarship. It was this civil regulation of the social relationships of student life that provided the measure in terms of which the impact of government policy on certain groups could be judged unfair. Although it was the experience of difference that our students most appreciated in each other, that sense of difference was attached to an awareness of the importance of equity in other respects, and it was the disturbance of that equity that they identified as unjust. Policies were judged not simply in terms of how they affected individuals personally but also in terms of their impact upon others and upon some shared awareness of a common moral order. These things are significant for citizenship in that they at least echo or resonate with wider and deeper historical features of the development of civil society as the bedrock of citizenship.

We argued that it is possible for people to have a sense of being civil, of being members of a public civil society, without their being involved in 'official politics' in the formal sense. Scepticism towards the state does not necessarily imply a general apathy or privatised withdrawal from the social. Furthermore, this condition has a firm foundation in the history of citizenship and its origins in the public sphere. In the first instance, citizenship has to do with the relationship between citizen and citizen rather than between citizen and government. Those more recent historical studies utilising Habermas' model of the public sphere extend it in various ways: in time and space, but also in social complexity. Sequentially, the public sphere can be seen as having been conceptualised in three distinct ways. In the first case, Habermas' model is an illuminating and highly suggestive idealisation that is substantively restricted in historical and social scope: a bourgeois, male public sphere based in the predominantly literary culture of the late eighteenth-century coffee-houses of England and France. The second phase encompassed critiques that extended the social range of the public sphere to include plebeian and female spheres, but which did so through reductive analyses that take *identity* as the constitutive principle. Here, the public sphere is restricted in terms of content and agenda, the key questions being: *whose* public sphere is it and what are their *interests?* Behind this approach stands a set of standpoint or interest theoretic perspectives. Third, in the cases we considered, the public sphere comes to be extended in time, space and social complexity, and in terms of structure and process rather than content and agenda. In much the way that the emergence of the public sphere marked a reflexivity that made modern society visible to itself, so in a further move, the public sphere becomes its own object of description. Against the reductionism of the earlier critiques of Habermas, this more recent approach grants the public sphere a principle of autonomy in its own right. It becomes a space whose principle regulates a particular mode of sociality in dealing with difference and justice. In the long run, history suggests, the public sphere is the space within which arguments for recognition, inclusion and equity of treatment can eventually be won, but the condition for this is that it remains a Great Republic and resists postmodern balkanisation. As Blanning says, 'What matters about it is not what it contains in terms of ideas or feelings or even its social composition, but the fact that those concerns are actively communicated' (2002: 8–9). It is this 'effort of communication' that is the crucial process identified by the writers we reviewed and that can also be associated with the sociality of student life.

It can be claimed, then, that being a student involves the refinement of a 'praxis of personal and social adjustment' (Porter 2000: 22) in relation to others and their differences and conditions. In a period of significant university expansion, the contribution of the university to citizenship and the public sphere becomes especially significant. If it indeed becomes the case that 50 per cent of school-leavers will progress to higher education, then the sociality of student life will be experienced by a considerable proportion of the population. It is not our intention to embark at this point upon an extended discussion of the university in a period of expansion and of considerable social change, but it is important to at least register the importance of identifying and preserving those qualities of the university that not only sustain but might positively enhance the sense of mutuality and reinvigorate the currently attenuated relationship between civil society and the political process. In historical terms, as we observed, citizenship and the sociality of the public sphere were intrinsically linked with the emergence of modes of critical liberal scholarship. But these codes were not invariably lodged within the universities. In the key formative period of citizenship and the public sphere, they were in significant respects being formalised outside the university, as much in scientific as in literary culture and in homes as well as in public places. As Delanty (2000) has pointed out, the university today no longer monopolises knowledge production in the way that it might be seen as having done in much the nineteenth and twentieth centuries (though not in the seventeenth and eighteenth). Although knowledge is ever more central in the 'knowledge society' it is also more diffuse. What the university preserves, however, is a central role as 'a site of interconnectivity ... [and] communication becomes more central to it' (Delanty 2000: 7–8). This 'more communicative concept of the university', he suggests could define the contemporary mission of the university: 'The university must recover the public space of discourse that has been lost in the decline of the public sphere' (ibid.: 7). These brief observations are both speculative and tentative, but serve to indicate the manner in which a cluster of concepts and concerns across a range of otherwise disconnected scholarly work might be drawn together to form a new lens and intellectual matrix through which to approach the issue of citizenship.

Our decision to approach citizenship from a partially different direction, reflected a sense that the more conventional approaches through the political process and issues of participation were not only repetitive but missing something that could at least be sensed in our day-to-day dealings with students and in the teaching and social contexts of university life. Although certainly conscious of their general lack of interest in or engagement with the political process and its issues, to describe them as consequently 'apathetic' misses an important quality that enlivens their relationship with each other, their teachers and the knowledge with which they are engaging. One advantage of the 'oblique' method we adopted in our study was that it enabled us to access this quality which we are now associating here with a civil sense of mutuality and a distinct mode of sociality. On this basis, the relationship to the formal political process is, perhaps, better described as quiescent rather than apathetic (it is certainly not acquiescent). To approach citizenship from the perspective of the civil rather than the political is to retrace the primary relationship in the historical development of citizenship and to remind ourselves of its bedrock. In this more positive posture, an extended investigation of education, the university and the public sphere under current historical conditions might provide fresh insights to aid the reinvigoration of formal participatory democracy.

6.4 Fears

Having recognised all this, it is also possible, however, to see the space in which these students live and talk as educated, caring, socially aware citizens as fragile. Their particular situation seems in various respects temporary. At the personal level, being a student is a transitional state and can be a respite from the demands of 'normal' everyday life. And historically, for our interviewees, being students during the period 1998 to 2001 meant they were living through a moment of transition – the end of the grant system. What we have called the fragility of the situation can be appreciated by considering both the financial conditions of most of the students in this group, and what appears to be the currently unstable method of funding their universities. These students have in fact received continuing, substantial support from the state, both in the way taxes have paid for at least three-quarters of their tuition costs and also currently guarantee their loans at levels of interest well below those found in the market-place. Their two quite different universities have been charging the same level of fees, with the effect that tuition costs to individuals of taking a three-year degree course at APU and the University of Cambridge are roughly the same. It is perhaps a problem, however, that few were aware of this support received from general taxation and fewer still were able to accurately estimate its extent. What most were conscious of and did appreciate was the way in which their parents or partners were sustaining them. One could say that, for many, this space in which they were able to articulate a sense of caring citizenship seems objectively to have been a space protected by what they acknowledge as *private*, intergenerational transfers. From the point of view of the providers (the parents and partners), this support appears to be motivated by humanistic values of caring and it depends upon considerable levels of trust. The way the support was received and used reflected those values. In the language of some recent Third Way educational theorising one could say that these families have been major generators of social capital for these students.

But it is here where the overall situation is so problematic. It is threatened by two inter-related developments. First, there is the possibility of further differentiation and privatisation of the costs of higher education. So-called 'top-up fees', for example, would add a further financially differentiating element to an already somewhat *culturally* divided university system. If we believe what these students have told us, 'top up fees' would further narrow the recruitment base of high status institutions. If loans remain in place, it can always be argued that those from less well-off families can still go to such institutions and pay back the extra later. However, this depends upon those students and their families accepting the kinds of life and work which such large repayments require. As we have seen in the responses of students within one such high status institution, a sizeable group *reject* such destinations in favour of public service. Such institutions, within a university system highly differentiated by fees, could prove to be exclusive by destination as well as origin and thus, *inter alia*, diminish the chances of what we have called mutual political learning (Section 4.6) as well as the wider sense of mutuality discussed in Chapter 5.

Second, it may be argued that such social differentiation between institutions would not occur because of the ways parents and partners support students by private transfers. This might indeed be the case for some, but relatively minor economic changes could so easily undermine the ability of large numbers of middle-income parents to help their children as student-citizens in the non-instrumental ways we have seen. This private ability to help fund higher education depends upon economic conditions which maintain current levels of full-time employment of the providers and part-time employment for the students themselves. It also depends in most cases upon increases in the value of assets held passively by many, in pension funds, savings and investments. As both privatisation of pensions and the financing of higher education proceeds, inter-age transfers come to depend more and more upon the vagaries of markets in financial assets, rises in shareholder value, and increases in the value of domestic property.

It remains to be seen whether the mutualities, civilities and generosity born of student life and family support may prove fragile as these things come to depend increasingly upon favourable personal and private circumstances.

6.5 Citizenship education?

As we noted at the beginning of this chapter, the initial impetus for writing this book came from an interest in two apparently unconnected policy developments: the introduction of tuition fees and loans within higher education, and the establishment of Citizenship as a Foundation Subject within the National Curriculum. It seems appropriate, therefore, to conclude our discussion with some assessment of what citizenship education in England and Wales may portend now that the subject is mandatory in all English secondary schools at Key Stages 3 and 4.

A quite substantial body of commentary has accumulated concerning the *motives* underlying the decision to introduce citizenship education at this point in time, following decades of official neglect or half-hearted commitment. We shall discuss here a number of these accounts. In Section 6.2, we have ourselves suggested one interpretation: that highlighting citizenship as part of the *content* of education could be seen as a convenient way of adding a social gloss to an education system which was being reshaped structurally in ways which reinforce individualistic instrumentalism. On this view, establishing citizenship education enables government to profess its concern with the centrality of citizenship while many of its actual policies, both within and beyond education, are contributing to a further *dismantling* of social citizenship. From this perspective, the very ambiguity surrounding what 'citizenship' means can be seen as politically convenient.

Other commentators have gone further. Gamarnikow and Green (2000) have claimed that the *kind* of citizenship education the government is promoting is calculated to undermine Marshallian social citizenship in favour of various kinds of voluntarism. They interpret this as consistent with Third Way policy rhetoric which seeks to foreground certain conceptions of social capital – notably those involving voluntarism, individual moral responsibility, and family and social networks as key sources for the revitalisation of civil society. They argue that the authors of the Crick Report (Advisory Group on Citizenship 1998) systematically *disregard* those forms of social capital which, as in Bourdieu's use of the concept, emphasise social *in*equalities and unequal access to social networks which confer advantage, and that instead the report treats 'social capital as an unproblematically egalitarian social glue'. Gamarnikow and Green warn that 'this opens up a potentially dangerous space for the deepening of political complacency, absolving the state from responsibility for economic and political regeneration, while locating the socially well-placed as resources with obligations for renewing civil society' (2000: 109–10). They contrast this with Marshall's social citizenship in the following terms:

> While recognising the importance of voluntary associations and a mixed economy of welfare, Marshall's social citizenship located moral and political responsibility for welfare and social justice in the nation state. It was social citizenship and rights of social justice which 'civilised' society. By contrast, the Crick Report locates the argument for community involvement in the changing balance between state provision of welfare and community and individual responsibility. In other words, Marshall's social citizenship as a site for welfare rights disappears and its place is now occupied by duties of volunteering and community involvement. The Crick Report

> constructs the Third Way citizen whose individual and civic responsibility enables the Third Way state to provide opportunities rather than services.
>
> (ibid.: 106)

It is debatable whether this analysis is entirely fair to Crick himself; in particular, the interpretation of 'political literacy' as 'primarily instrumental' (ibid.: 106). But their argument that the Crick Report's stress on active citizenship tends to construct both alienation and abstentionism as 'deficits of knowledge and understanding rather than as engendered by institutional inadequacies' (ibid.) is well made, and chimes strongly with certain aspects of our own account (especially in Chapter 5).

We shall shortly consider further Gamarnikow and Green's central argument about voluntarism displacing social citizenship. But before doing so, it is important to point out that these authors are by no means alone in discerning the not-so-hidden hand of New Labour and Third Way ideology as a shaping influence on the citizenship education proposals. Several prominent *conservative* thinkers have also detected what they see as biases of this kind. Anthony O'Hear attacked the citizenship education proposals on the very day that they were launched, contending that:

> One can see why a government of lawyers, modernisers and professional politicians might like the idea of citizenship education. It is a way of making the next generation the same type of people as they are. But for the rest of us, that is a reason for resisting the very idea.
>
> (O'Hear 1999)

Anthony Flew (2000) has similarly detected political bias in the government's orientation to citizenship education, seeing it, *inter alia*, as potentially a vehicle through which the government's Europhile agenda is likely to be promoted. Flew castigates the Advisory Group on Citizenship for what he sees as the scandalous neglect in its Final Report of 'the implications of the European Union project for British citizenship' (ibid.: 32) and asserts that 'the administration under which this Advisory Group was established has already conducted an historically unprecedented campaign of (pro-EU) political indoctrination in British schools' (ibid.: 35). O'Hear similarly detects a clear pro-EU bias: 'citizenship education is ... a means of getting young people into a state of mind where they are hungry for continuous political and social change, and perhaps eventually for the ultimate change: acceptance of a federal Europe' (1999). Another prominent right-wing commentator, James Tooley (2000), has also discerned political bias in the Crick Report – 'it is pretty easy to spot a tad of political bias creeping in at every stage' (ibid.: 145) – though Tooley does *not* identify the systematic promotion of a Third Way agenda.

How should we assess such attributions of political motivation and interest? And even if we were to consider certain of them well founded, does this mean that citizenship education *as implemented* is likely to have the effects suggested? We shall focus here on certain of the questions raised by Gamarnikow and Green, since these are most closely connected to the issues we have been addressing throughout this book. Once again, we find ourselves faced with both hopes and fears. In terms of hopes, there are some reasons for believing that whatever the political motivations behind the introduction of citizenship education may have been, no strong political 'line' or ideology is likely to be *promoted* in schools. It is clear that most of those concerned with implementation, whether at the policy or school levels, are highly conscious of the risks (and accusations) of political bias, and that they are likely to take pains to try to ensure that Citizenship is taught in an educationally responsible way which respects the rationality and the autonomy of students. The Crick Report devotes considerable attention to the ways in which citizenship education is not only controversial in itself but recurrently involves *issues* which are controversial in character. At an early stage, the Advisory Group set up a sub-group chaired by Dr Alex Porter to address precisely these concerns, and Section 10 of the Final Report offers substantial guidance about how schools might deal with controversial matters, as well as summarising the statutory requirements of the 1996 Education Act about the treatment of controversial issues in schools (Advisory Group on Citizenship 1998: 56–61). Such advice is reiterated and elaborated in a number of the guidance documents and materials which the Qualifications and Curriculum Authority has produced since then (see, for example, QCA 2000, 2001). Furthermore, such research evidence as we possess about the attitudes of *teachers* in these respects strongly suggests that the great majority are only too conscious of how these aspects of citizenship education may be perceived by parents, governors, and other interested parties, and of how sections of the media periodically sensationalise and misrepresent schools' attempts to deal with controversial issues (e.g. Arnot *et al.* 1995; Davies *et al.* 1999). Such sensitivities, indeed, are probably one of the main reasons why many teachers continue to have strong reservations about becoming involved in curriculum areas of this kind.

Yet it may be for these very reasons that forms of citizenship education could emerge which might well, albeit unintentionally, have the kinds of effects to which Gamarnikow and Green point. It is very possible that a number of influences could converge to bring about forms of relatively 'depoliticised' citizenship education which might implicitly reinforce a politics which prioritises 'community', the importance of individual 'contributions' in building certain kinds of social capital, voluntary participation, etc. – and lead to a corresponding neglect of arguments about the role of the state in relation to social citizenship and citizenship entitlements.

In the first place, Gamarnikow and Green may well be right to argue that the definition of citizenship education set out in the Crick Report may itself 'steer' practice in schools in the directions we (and they) have identified. The report placed equal emphasis on three 'inter-related' dimensions of citizenship education: 'social and moral responsibility, community involvement, and political literacy'; moreover 'political literacy' was glossed in this section of the report as 'pupils learning how to make themselves effective in public life through knowledge, skills and values' (Advisory Group on Citizenship 1998: 13). Now, although elsewhere, Crick himself has foregrounded political literacy much more strongly and has emphasised the role of critical understanding of political issues and concepts as being central to it (e.g. Crick 2000a: Chapters 4 and 5), the report itself may well convey a different order of priorities. Moreover, the Citizenship Programmes of Study arguably reinforce this message. In the first place, the term 'political literacy' disappears in favour of a content-heavy list of elements which 'pupils should be taught about'. Second, responsible pupil participation in school and community based activities becomes mandatory (Department for Education and Employment and the Qualifications and Curriculum Authority 1999: 15–16). And there is evidence that this strong emphasis on community participation was influenced by the direct intervention of Secretary of State David Blunkett. Crick's own account of the processes of drafting the Citizenship Order reveals that 'the Secretary of State sent word to the working party ... that actual participation could be mandatory, if we cared so to recommend; we did not demur' (Crick 2000a: 119). The combination of this kind of 'steer', a content-heavy list of information to be acquired, and schools' and teachers' understandable caution about handling matters that are politically controversial could well all work together to encourage a combination of 'safe civics' and the limited kinds of 'active citizenship' which centre on young people's voluntary participation in school and community.

The chief danger is that this combination is the recipe with which many schools and parents will feel most comfortable – especially in the context of a political climate and associated policy developments which are subtly but steadily pushing ever further in the directions Gamarnikow and Green identify. Tony Blair's (1996) 'Stakeholder Society' speech set the tone from the outset – where he argued that a stake in education involved a combination of 'inclusiveness with individuality ... [and] reflects the wider synthesis of community and individual ... [which] is the essential underpinning of New Labour's approach' (Blair 1996: 304). In this same speech, he highlighted the importance of community as follows:

> successful communities are about what people give as much as what they take, and any attempt to rebuild community for a modern age must assert that personal and social responsibility are not optional extras ... we owe duty to more than the self.
>
> (ibid.: 304, cited in Rose 1999b)

In more recent speeches, Blair and other ministers have steadily reiterated the rhetoric of 'enabling government' in partnership both with those who are prepared to be responsibly active within civil society, at the same time also emphasising the vital role of public–private partnerships. In a key speech in 1998, Blair spelt out, perhaps more explicitly than ever before, his view of the links between certain kinds of active citizenship, the strengthening of civil society, self-help, social capital, and a 'modernised' form of social democracy:

> We can only realise ourselves as individuals in a thriving civil
> society, comprising strong families and civic institutions but-
> tressed by intelligent government ... Whether in education,
> health, social work, crime prevention or the care of children,
> 'enabling' government strengthens civil society ... and helps
> families and communities improve their own performance ...
> This is the Third Way – a modernised social democracy for a
> changing world which will build its prosperity on human and
> social capital.
>
> (Blair 1998: 3, 14, 20, cited in
> Gamarnikow and Green 2000: 96)

We cannot here itemise the succession of policy changes since
1997 that can be seen as consistent with this orientation, for
example, the preoccupation with social capital formation as a key
means of combating 'social exclusion'. For the purposes of our
discussion, one recent example will have to suffice: the government's active encouragement of the development of both
Specialist Schools and Faith Schools.[1] Such policies have been
'sold' as involving a virtuous combination of enhanced consumer
choice, strengthened family life, and reinforcement of the traditional moral bonds underpinning certain local communities.
Unfortunately though, it seems more than plausible, especially
within the wider context we have described, that schools of this
kind will have a natural affinity with those approaches to political
education which accentuate – quite as much through the wider
school ethos as the taught curriculum – orientations which subtly
reinforce circumscribed forms of localised 'active citizenship'
while fighting shy of more fundamental and more controversial
political debates focused on the *nation* and competing views of
national citizenship and citizenship rights. In such a context, the
absence of a strong language and consciousness of citizenship
may further reinforce such convenient myopia.

The data from our interviews could be seen as in some ways
supporting such forebodings, although once again, we are in a
realm of speculation since we are imagining the situation of our
respondents as *parents*. There is, first, the sense of fatalism displayed by many of our students about the inevitability of further
privatisation and privatism, even as they simultaneously sustained
moral reservations about it. Second, the very sense of civility that
supports treating others in a civil manner may also be conducive

to the view that one should not stand in the way of others' success or seek to prevent them doing what they will with their own money. This may also resonate with a British tradition of politeness and reticence in which making disagreement too overt is seen as 'bad form' and an offence against civility. Finally, those in families in which one partner works in the private sector (often securing benefits of private health insurance and the like) while the other is in public service may be peculiarly tempted, especially when facing 'hard choices', to sometimes and understandably favour private solutions. Such parents may, again quite 'naturally', feel most at ease with forms of political education that do not pose too many uncomfortable questions.

Overall, the prospects for a form of citizenship education that might connect the underlying sense of mutuality and social concern that was so evident among our respondents with a commitment to a national politics, which puts social citizenship decisively back on the agenda, do not seem promising.

Appendix
Student profiles

Anglia Polytechnic University

Peter

Aged 37, Peter was completing his BA in Sociology and Politics and hoped to proceed to a higher degree. He is a mature student who had been in Local Education Authority employment for ten years before embarking on his degree course. Sources of finance for his studies were mainly from his own work and savings, the Student Loan, and the Dependants Grant – with a small contribution from his former partner.

Andy

Aged 32 and at the end of his Sociology and Politics course, Andy had rather indefinite plans for the future but was looking for a job that was intrinsically interesting rather than highly paid. He came from a rural community in SW England. The costs of his degree were financed chiefly from loans, supplemented to a small extent by help from family and income from his own earnings.

Tony

Aged 30, Tony was completing his undergraduate course in single honours Sociology, after which his career plans were uncertain, though he had considered taking either a master's degree or perhaps a PGCE at another university. Since leaving school at 16, he had worked in commerce in what he saw as a routine job. Tony had taken out the maximum student loan every year and had supplemented this from his own earnings with small occasional contributions from various family members.

Laura

Aged 28, Laura was reading single honours Sociology and as a result of her success on the course had developed a strong motivation to pursue a career locally in research. She had given up a relatively well-paid job to become a full-time student and had financed her course through a combination of full student loans, vacation earnings and substantial contributions from her partner.

Matt

Aged 21, Matt, an overseas student, was completing a combined honours degree in Sociology and History, and was planning to go on to a master's degree in a field oriented towards business or politics. Matt indicated that about 80 per cent of the costs of his taking the course had come from his family and the remainder from his own earnings and savings but as a student from the EU, his tuition fees had been paid from public funds.

Samantha

Aged 22, Samantha was reading combined honours Sociology and Women's Studies. She had ambitions to follow this with an MA, funding permitting, and then a primary PGCE course in Cambridge. Samantha began her course before the introduction of tuition fees and full student loans and therefore felt she had a relatively low level of debt which was almost entirely in the form of the Student Loan.

Jasmine

A mature student aged 44, married and with children, Jasmine was completing her degree in Sociology and hoped in due course to take a professional social work qualification. She started her course before the introduction of tuition fees and had financed her studies partly through the Student Loan and partly from her own savings and earnings, though she also stressed the significance of her husband's earnings in providing support for the family throughout her period of study.

Anita

Aged 20, Anita was completing a joint honours degree in Sociology and Criminology. Anita's career plans were still indefinite though she had undertaken work experience placements, for example, with the police service. She had taken out the full student loan over three years and expected to pay this off herself, but her parents had funded the cost of tuition fees and provided other kinds of financial support.

Sara

Aged 21, Sara had been studying for a joint honours degree in Sociology and Politics and had definite plans to go on to take a master's degree in Criminology. Sara stressed the importance of the strong moral support which, as a child of an Asian family and member of the Asian community, she had received throughout her course. She had financed her undergraduate studies mainly via the Student Loan with some contribution from her own earnings but expected to receive financial support from her family for her projected postgraduate studies – support which she planned to repay when circumstances permitted.

Lydia

Aged 28, Lydia was completing a single honours degree in Sociology; she had worked for ten years in a magazine publishing company before starting her degree. At the end of her courses she hoped to seek employment in the field of human resources management/adult training; she also stressed that there was likely to be a geographical limitation on her job applications in order to fit in with the demands of her partner's employment and she indicated her willingness to follow his career moves, at least until she had obtained steady employment after graduating. She had financed her undergraduate course largely via the Student Loan, with small contributions from her own earnings and from her partner who had also paid a higher proportion of domestic expenses during the course of her degree.

Delphine

Aged 24, Delphine was completing her BA in Health, Welfare and

Social Policy, having previously been a student for two years elsewhere; she planned to follow her first degree with an MA in the same area, having at the time of the interview already obtained some measure of grant support for this. In the longer term, she hoped to work in a public sector post, probably in the UK but possibly in the EU. She had begun her studies before tuition fees were introduced, and the other costs of her degree were roughly equally divided between the Student Loan, support from her parents, and her own earnings, with a small contribution from an access fund.

Jonathan

A mature student aged 48, Jonathan was completing a degree in Social Policy and hoped to follow this with a master's course at a university in the Midlands. He had begun his undergraduate course as a part-time student, paying the costs from his own earnings and only becoming a full-time student in his final year. He had taken out no loans at any stage, financing most of the costs of his course from his own savings and earnings, though with significant contributions from his partner.

Grace

Aged 32, Grace was a mature student reading for a joint honours degree in Forensic Science and Criminology; she hoped to pursue a career in the area of forensic science, possibly having taken a master's degree first. Grace had worked for twelve years in administrative and office jobs and, following redundancy, had decided to reorient her career by taking a degree with a vocational emphasis. She had financed her career entirely from student loans, regarding it as important to devote all her time to her studies while at university.

Cambridge University

Anne

Aged 22, Anne is a student finishing her BEd degree. She comes from a family of teachers, living in a rural area of East Anglia. Her higher education has been financed by loans and parental help.

She was applying for a teaching post herself when interviewed, in order to be with her boyfriend.

Helen

Aged 22, and at the end of her BEd course, Helen's parents were the chief source of funds for the four years she has spent in Cambridge, with some part-time earnings. She had no loans. Both parents had small businesses of their own. She planned to work as a teacher for a short while, have a family, and then return to teaching later.

Margaret

Margaret was just completing a Cambridge BEd degree funded by a combination of loans, part-time earnings, and a bursary. Aged 22, she was from a farming family and her immediate plans were to travel abroad and do temporary jobs, and 'I'll worry about the rest of my life later' as she put it.

Lyn

Aged 22, she was completing her BEd degree and had secured a place as a teacher in a primary school. She was returning to her home area and, initially, planned to live with her parents who were both teachers. Lyn had funded her HE by a combination of grants, parental help and part-time earnings. Loans have been taken out but invested.

Susan

Aged 22, Susan is a veterinary student who has just completed her first tripos in Social and Political Sciences at Cambridge University. She plans to go on and do the next three years of the clinical Part II of the tripos in veterinary practice. She was unsure about whether she would become a vet after that. So far, Susan has been helped by her parents who have paid for food and rent, and has student loans and an overdraft. She has also worked part-time.

Marion

Aged 22, Marion is just finishing her Cambridge University BA Hons in Social and Political Sciences. She is hoping to go on to study for an MA in town planning. If her degree results are good enough she will get a scholarship. As she had taken a sabbatical year to be an officer in the students' union she was still receiving a grant. Her parents have also helped to fund her higher education and she had worked during most holidays.

Luke

Aged 21, Luke had just completed his Cambridge University BA course in Social and Political Sciences. He has applied for graduate trainee schemes with *The Times* and the BBC and hoped to have a long-term career in international journalism. He has been supported financially by his family throughout the course and has no loans. His father was a graduate.

Harriet

Aged 21, Harriet is just completing her BA in Social and Political Sciences at Cambridge University where she has been offered a place to do an MPhil in Criminology, depending upon her results. At the time of the interview she was also looking at another master's degree course in Social Policy and Social Work at Oxford University. She hopes to work after that in international development or charity administration. Harriet had funded her degree from a mix of family help, loans, an overdraft, and part-time earnings. Her father is a vicar and her mother a head-teacher.

Francesca

Francesca is a Cambridge University Economics student. She is from Germany where her parents still live and has been offered a job by a large international finance house in a major German city. She hopes to be transferred to the London office in due course. Both her parents went to university and she describes them as being more academic than she is.

Philip

Philip is a Cambridge University Economics student. He comes from a working-class family in a major English industrial city. Both his parents started working at fifteen immediately on leaving school. He had expected to leave school after GCSE and become a 'mechanic', but his very good results persuaded him to do A levels and then apply to Cambridge. He has been offered a post as a business analyst with a major company in London.

Carolyn

Carolyn is studying English and Drama with Education Studies in Cambridge University. Her intention is to go into event management where she thinks she can use her social and personal skills to good effect. She values her degree for its breadth which she sees as relevant to her career plans.

Kelvin

Kelvin is studying English and Drama with Education Studies in Cambridge University. He is the first in his family to go to university, but his father gained technical qualifications through part-time study and his mother is a nurse. He intends to be a teacher though he thinks he will probably change profession after ten or fifteen years if he becomes 'burnt out'. He has some regrets about not having done an apprenticeship. High earnings are not his priority and he chose his course on the basis of interest. As a deferred student, he did not have to pay tuition fees.

Abigail

Abigail is studying Education Studies at Cambridge University and intends to go into development work overseas as a teacher. She also intends to return to university at some point to study for a higher degree. Although a British national, her parents live in Switzerland and she and they have borne the cost of her degree. She defines herself as 'left-wing'. Both her parents did degrees in Britain.

Denise

Denise is studying Biological Sciences with Education Studies in

Cambridge University. She is going on to do an MPhil in Environment and Development. Her aim is to work overseas for a Christian development agency planning agricultural systems. She does not expect a high income. Her father is a dentist and her mother a doctor.

Emily

Emily is taking a degree in Education Studies at Cambridge University. She hopes to continue on to the MPhil degree and eventually a PhD with the aim of becoming a lecturer. She had initially wanted to be a school teacher, but decided that becoming an academic was more to her liking. Her father does not have a degree, but her mother does and is now doing a PGCE.

Melanie

Melanie is studying English and Drama with Education Studies at Cambridge University. Her aim is to go into youth work in the community. She is also interested in film work and would like to be able to combine the two areas. She has experience in youth and community work already. Both her parents left school at fifteen but also later trained to become youth workers, and her mother gained an Open University degree.

Robert

Robert is studying Geography with Education Studies in Cambridge University. He has been offered a job at a city bank. He hopes to be able to work abroad for a couple of years. He worked in a school in New Zealand in his gap year. Both his parents trained as teachers in Zimbabwe and he is very conscious of the much wider range of opportunities he enjoys relative to them.

Grant

Grant is studying English with Education Studies in Cambridge University and has been offered a job with a large firm of solicitors in London. He will take a law conversion course for the first two years. His original intention had been to study law, but he decided to follow this degree instead out of interest and then convert. He hopes to spend some years in America. His father trained as a dentist in the army and his mother was not allowed to continue her education past O level. Both his parents have been highly encouraging of his own educational career.

Notes

1 Citizenship in Britain: models and identities

1 The phrase is, of course, that of E. P. Thompson (1965).
2 This alerts us to the important point that many theoretically elaborated conceptions of citizenship are strongly *normative*: this applies equally to Marshallian and neo-liberal conceptions as well as to the work of political philosophers as diverse as Sandel, MacIntyre, John Rawls or John Gray. A properly sociological treatment and definition of citizenship, while not of course value-free, has the potential advantage of being able to relate such normative theories to their grounding in social, economic and political conditions.
3 This opens onto a large and contested terrain. David Miller, for example, who distinguishes three kinds of citizenship pertinent to the UK (liberal/Marshallian, citizens as consumers of public services, and active citizenship), argues: 'My own view concerning this matter is controversial. We cannot have active citizenship in the modern world, without inclusive national identities to support it.' He goes on to suggest that some form of 'nested citizenship' may emerge to contain a more flexible and inclusive understanding of nationality but adds: 'But at the same time, we must recognise that we cannot teach people to be citizens without teaching them to be members of a national community' (Miller 2000a: 31).
4 David Miller adumbrates a similar if more narrowly focused vision of 'the citizen as a consumer of public services who therefore has consumers' rights', and who is 'empowered to expect a certain standard of service or provision, and empowered to seek compensation or redress if the service is not satisfactory' (Miller 2000a: 28). Miller's primary interest, however, is in contrasting this citizen (who is recognised as 'active' but only in limited ways) with the more authentically 'active citizen' of the civic republican tradition, for example, as this term is interpreted by Bernard Crick (Crick 2000a: 8, 2000b: 6).
5 It is arguable that Rose's whole analysis of the reconstitution of citizenship under what he calls 'advanced liberalism' is perhaps too closed, too neat, too programmatic, constructed as it is from the standpoint of an attempt to persuade us that we are witnessing an

epochal shift in paradigms of governmentality. This is not to deny, of course, that his post-structuralist stance does leave theoretical space for the construction of alternative and dissenting lifestyles and identities (see Rose 1999b: 489–91).

6 This form of explanation has affinities with Moore's (1996) explanatory account of the steadily increasing educational success of girls as compared with boys in the UK. Moore argues that the most visible interventions to promote gender equality, i.e. feminist equal opportunities initiatives internal to schooling, actually had *weak* effects on differential attainment as compared with the less visible and longer-term operation of systemic phenomena external to education. The idea of 'invisible' citizenship also has affinities with Bernstein's notions of invisible pedagogies (Bernstein 1977).

7 Thatcher sought to disavow class as alien and unBritish, insisting that it 'is a communist concept. It groups people as bundles and sets them against one another' (Thatcher 1992: 37, cited in Cannadine 1998: 2).

8 'even passports have only referred to their holders as *citizens* rather than *subjects* since, appropriately, their jackets have turned from blue to red' (Miller 2000a: 26).

9 The rise of the 'satire boom' in the 1960s was probably in part another symptom of this growing sense that the old forms and imagery of hierarchy had been rendered ridiculous in a changed world.

10 Pimlott points out that the Beveridge Report, whose 'snazzy title' was *Social Insurance and Allied Services: Report Presented to Parliament by Command of his Majesty* (1942) rapidly became a best-seller and 'the queue to buy copies was reputedly a mile long and sales reached a hundred thousand within a month of its publication' (Pimlott 1992).

11 The role of wartime conditions in contributing to a transformation in public acceptance of a greatly expanded role for the state in welfare provision is highlighted in the following summarising comments by Richard Titmuss:

> It would in any relative sense be true to say that by the end of the Second World War the Government had, through the agency of newly established or existing services, assumed and developed a measure of direct concern for the health and well-being of the population which, by contrast with the role of Government in the nineteen-thirties, was little short of remarkable. No longer did concern rest on the belief that, in respect of many social needs it was proper to intervene only to assist the poor and those who were unable to pay for services of one kind and another. Instead, it was increasingly regarded as a proper function or even obligation of Government to ward off distress and strain among not only the poor but almost all classes of society.
>
> (Titmuss 1950: 506)

12 In the middle of the Blitz, Mass Observation investigated 'the political and related changes that people expected to emerge as a result of the

new "total" war'. These data too indicate that substantial numbers of people were anticipating significant shifts in the direction of what would later become recognised as a social democratic agenda (see Hennessy 1993: 77; Harrison 1976: 314–15).

13 In this sense, these changes were another aspect of 'the end of deference' – uncomfortable as this may have been for many professional employees in state-provided services.

2 Prospects for social national citizenship in the UK

1 Our use of citizenship does not, however, commit us to all aspects of Heater's citizenship ideal. Citizenship for us need not, for example, depend upon the fostering (or the existence) of the sort of pervasive active citizenship associated with the civic republican tradition. This is a key part of Heater's vision and also underlies Bernard Crick's successful efforts to establish citizenship *education* as an element of the National Curriculum in England. Discussing the Report of the Advisory Group on Citizenship which he chaired, Crick has written: 'there is a philosophy behind the Report of course: what scholars call civic republicanism and also pluralism' (Crick 2000a: 120).

2 For a robust, succinct and *philosophically* informed defence of positive rights to consensually agreed levels of provision of health care, social security and education, see Raymond Plant's 'Citizenship and Rights' (1990). This penetrating essay offers a sustained critique of a range of neo-liberal arguments on these issues.

3 The IPPR is the left-leaning 'think tank': the Institute for Public Policy Research.

4 It is neither irrelevant nor accidental that private health insurance was being offered as part of the 'remuneration package' for new teachers in a number of London schools as a response to the crisis of teacher recruitment in 2001–2. However, it is also worth noting that the issue of the *Daily Telegraph* which carried Janet Daley's provocative attack on Matthew Taylor also carried, on its front page, an article pointing out that 'rising property prices are denying many people the chance to join the housing ladder' with the result that 'in some towns and cities essential services were at risk because key workers such as teachers and nurses could no longer afford to live there' (*Daily Telegraph*, 21 August 2001: 1). This article was based on a survey by the National Housebuilding Federation.

5 A recent case in point is John Petrovic's argument that adherence to principles of democracy in schools requires not only the positive portrayal of homosexuality within the school but also precludes teachers from expressing their beliefs against it (Petrovic 1999). For a rejoinder, see Beck (2001).

6 The following statement made to the Bradford Commission in 1996 and quoted in the Parekh Report (Runnymede Trust 2000) indicates the way in which, in modern Britain, it is possible for British citizens to live relatively comfortably with a kaleidoscope of identities without finding this disorientating:

I could view myself as a member of the following communities, depending on the context and in no particular order: Black, Asian, Azad Kashmiri, Mirpuri, Jat, Marilail, Kungriwalay, Pakistani, English, British, Yorkshireman, Bradfordian, from Bradford Moor ... I could use the term 'community' in any of these contexts and it would have meaning. Any attempt to define me as one of these would be meaningless.

(Bradford Commission 1996: 92; Runnymede Trust 2000: 47–8)

7 It was perhaps something of a hostage to fortune that in urging the need to 're-imagine' the meaning of nationhood in modern Britain, one short section of the Report suggested that while 'whiteness nowhere features as an explicit condition of being British ... it is widely understood that Englishness, and therefore by extension Britishness, is racially coded' (Runnymede Trust 2000: para. 3.20). This short section not only became the target of a barrage of hostile criticism, it also diverted attention from the crucial point that the vision of citizenship set out in the Report as a whole was one which strongly endorsed the role of a strong 'civic' national identity, summed up precisely in the phrase 'a community of communities *and a community of citizens*' (ibid.: 56, our italics).
8 The 'Irish question' is fraught with complexities and problems which we cannot enter into here.

3   Citizenship and the restructuring of higher education

1 The limits on community power within current arrangements for school organisation should not be under-estimated, see, for example, Deem *et al.* (1995) and Levacic (1995).

Part II Graduate citizens?

1 It is worth pointing out here that in all our interview data, there was only one occasion when a student spontaneously used the term 'citizen' – and even this was in response to a direct question:

INTERVIEWER: Do graduates have any obligations to anyone?
RESPONDENT: Do you mean me as British citizen or what?

6   Conclusion: concerns, hopes and fears

1 Although our interpretation of the effects of these policies for political education is inevitably speculative, the quantitative impact of the policies is likely to be considerable. The government's intention is that by 2004, at least one in seven secondary schools should be a Specialist School. And as far as Faith Schools are concerned, the current situation is as follows:

In the state sector (there are) 6,384 primary schools and 589 secondary schools; 4,716 Church of England, 2,100 Roman

Catholic, 27 Methodist, 32 Jewish, four Muslim, two Sikh, one
Greek Orthodox and one Seventh Day Adventist. The Muslim,
Sikh, Greek Orthodox, Seventh Day Adventist and five of the
Jewish schools have joined the state sector since 1997. Only four
of them are new schools: the rest have joined from the independ-
ent sector.

(*The Guardian*, 12 December 2001: 4)

The Anglican Church is actively pursuing plans to significantly
increase the number of its *secondary* schools and other faith
communities are being encouraged by government do likewise, e.g.
by reducing their contribution to the capital costs of school building
from 15 per cent to 10 per cent (ibid.).

Bibliography

Advisory Group on Citizenship (1998) *Education for Citizenship and the Teaching of Democracy in Schools: Final Report of the Advisory Group on Citizenship*, London: Department for Education and Employment/ Qualifications and Curriculum Authority.

Ahier, J. (1988) *Industry, Children and the Nation: An Analysis of National Identity in School Textbooks*, London: Falmer.

—— (2000) 'Financing Higher Education by Loans and Fees: Theorizing and Researching the Private Effects of a Public Policy', *Journal of Education Policy*, 15, 6: 683–700.

—— (2001) *Investing in Their Own Futures? Students, Their Parents, and Money: Choosing and Using Higher Education*, Project Research Paper 2, Milton Keynes: Open University.

Ainley, P. (1998) 'Towards a Learning or a Certified Society? Contradictions in the New Labour Modernization of Lifelong Learning', *Journal of Education Policy*, 13, 4: 559–73.

Alexander, J. C. (1995) *Fin de Siècle Social Theory: Relativism, Reduction and the Problem of Reason*, London: Verso.

Aristotle (1981) *The Politics* (revised edn. (ed.) T. J. Saunders), Harmondsworth: Penguin.

Arnot, M. (1997) 'Gendered Citizenry: New Feminist Perspectives on Education and Citizenship', *British Educational Research Journal*, 23, 3: 275–95.

Arnot, M., Dellyanni-Kouimtzis, K. and Ziogou, R. with Rowe, G. (1995) *Promoting Equality Awareness: Women as Citizens*, Final Report, June, Brussels: Equal Opportunities Unit, European Commission.

Ascherson, N. (1991) 'Only moneyed minies can afford to moan', *The Independent on Sunday*, 18 August: 18.

Association of University Teachers and the Development Education Association (1999) *Globalisation and Higher Education*, London: AUT and DEA.

Ball, S. J., Davies, J., David, M. and Reay, D. (2002) ' "Classification" and

"Judgement": social class and the "cognitive structures" of choice in Higher Education', *British Journal of Sociology of Education*, 23, 1: 51–72.

Barr, N. (1989) 'The White Paper on Student Loans', *Journal of Social Policy*, 18, 1: 409–17.

Bauman, Z. (1987) *Legislators and Interpreters: On Modernity, Post-modernity and Intellectuals*, Ithaca, NY: Cornell University Press.

—— (1995) *Life in Fragments: Essays in Postmodern Morality*, Oxford: Blackwell Publishers.

—— (1997) 'Universities: Old, New and Different', in A. Smith and F. Webster (eds) *The Postmodern University?*, Buckingham: Open University Press.

Beck, J. (1998) *Morality and Citizenship in Education*, London: Cassell.

—— (2001) 'Moral Democratic Education and Homosexuality: Censoring Morality, by John Petrovic, A Rejoinder', *Sex Education*, 1, 3: 235–44.

Beck, U. (1998) *Democracy Without Enemies*, Cambridge: Polity Press.

Bernstein, B. (1977) 'Class and Pedagogies: Visible and Invisible', in B. Bernstein *Class, Codes and Control*, vol. 3, 2nd edition, London: Routledge and Kegan Paul.

Blair, T. (1996) *New Britain: My Vision of a Young Country*, London: Fourth Estate.

—— (1998) *The Third Way: New Politics for the New Century*, London: The Fabian Society.

—— (2000) 'Education: The Story so Far', edited version of Romanes Lecture, *Prospect*, February: 9–12.

Blakey, M. (1994) 'Student Accommodation', in S. Haselgrove (ed.) *The Student Experience*, Buckingham: Society for Research into Higher Education and Open University Press.

Blanning, T. C. W. (2002) *The Culture of Power and the Power of Culture*, Oxford: Oxford University Press.

Blight, D., Davis, D. and Olsen, A. (1999) 'The Internationalisation of Higher Education', in K. Harry (ed) *Higher Education through Open and Distance Learning*, London: Routledge.

Blunkett, D. (2000) 'Radical Changes Will Prepare Higher Education for the 21st Century', press notice of speech at University of Greenwich, 15 February, Available: www.dfee.gov.uk.

Bradford Commission (1996) *The Bradford Commission Report*, London: The Stationery Office.

Britton, C. and Baxter, A. (1999) 'Becoming a Mature Student: Gendered Narratives of Self', *Gender and Education*, 11, 2: 179–93.

Callender, C. and Kemp, M. (2000) *Changing Student Finances: Income, Expenditure and the Take Up of Student Loans Among Full- and Part-time Students in 1998/9*, London: DFEE.

Campion, M. and Freeman, D. (1998) 'Globalization and Distance

Education Mega-institutions', in J. Currie and J. Newson (eds) *Universities and Globalization*, Thousand Oaks, CA: Sage Publications.

Cannadine, D. (1998) *Class in Britain*, New Haven, CT: Yale University Press.

Carnoy, M. (2000) 'Globalization and Educational Reform', in M. Stromquist and K. Monkman (eds) *Globalization and Education*, Lanham, MD: Rowman and Littlefield.

Cawkwell, J. and Pilkington, P. (1994) 'Rights and Representation', in S. Haselgrove (ed.) *The Student Experience*, Buckingham: The Society for Research into Higher Education and Open University Press.

Centre for Contemporary Cultural Studies (1981) *Unpopular Education: Schooling and Social Democracy in England Since 1944*, London: Hutchinson.

Chandler, J. (1998) *England in 1819*, Chicago: Chicago University Press.

Chen, S. (1999) *Citizens and Taxes*, London: The Fabian Society.

Citizen's Charter Unit (1992) *The Citizen's Charter: Raising the Standard*, London: Her Majesty's Stationery Office.

Clarke, J., Cochrane, A. and McLaughlin, E. (1994) 'Mission Accomplished or Unfinished Business? The Impact of Managerialization', in J. Clarke, A. Cochrane and E. McLaughlin (eds) *Managing Social Policy*, London: Sage.

Coles, R. (1986) *The Political Life of Children*, New York: The Atlantic Monthly Press.

Colley, L. (1986) 'Whose Nation? Class and National Consciousness in Britain 1750–1830', *Past and Present*, 11, 3: 115–27.

—— (1996) *Britons: Forging the Nation 1707–1937*, London: Vintage.

Commission on Taxation and Citizenship (2000) *Paying for Progress*, London: The Fabian Society.

Committee of Vice-Chancellors and Principals of the Universities of the UK (1999) *Making the Right Choice*, London: CVCP.

Committee on Higher Education (1963) *Higher Education*, Cmnd. 2154 (The Robbins Report), London: Her Majesty's Stationery Office.

Conover, P. J., Crewe, I. and Searing, D. (1991) 'The Nature of Citizenship in the United States and Great Britian: Empirical Comments on Theoretical Themes', *Journal of Politics*, 53: 800–32.

Crick, B. (2000a) *Essays on Citizenship*, London: Continuum.

—— (2000b) 'In Defence of the Citizenship Order', paper presented at the Political Studies Association UK 50th Annual Conference, 10–13 April, London.

Crouch, C. (2001) 'Citizenship and Markets in Recent British Education Policy', in C. Crouch, K. Eder and D. Tambini (eds) *Citizenship, Markets and the State*, Oxford: Oxford University Press.

Currie, J. and Newson, J. (eds) (1998) *Universities and Globalization*, Thousand Oaks, CA: Sage.

Dahrendorf, R. (1996) 'Citizenship and Social Class', in M. Bulmer and A. M. Rees (eds) *Citizenship Today: The Contemporary Relevance of T. H. Marshall*, London: University College London Press.

Daily Telegraph (2000) 'Straw Wants to Rewrite our History', 10 October: 1–2.

—— (2001) 'Key Workers Hit by House Prices', 21 August: 1.

Daley, J. (2001) 'The Road to Labour Utopia is Paved with Taxpayers' Money', *The Daily Telegraph*, 21 August: 19.

Davies, I., Gregory, I. and Riley, S. C. (1999) *Good Citizenship and Educational Provision*, London: Falmer Press.

Deem, R., Brehony, K. and Heath, S. (1995) *Active Citizenship and the Governing of Schools*, Buckingham: Open University Press.

Delanty, G. (2000) *Challenging Knowledge: The University in the Knowledge Society*, Buckingham: The Society for Research into Higher Education and the Open University Press.

Department for Education (1993) *The Charter for Higher Education*, London: DFE.

—— (1997) *Higher Education in the Learning Society* (The Dearing Report), London: Her Majesty's Stationery Office.

Department for Education and Employment (1998) *The Learning Age: A Renaissance for a New Britain*, Cmnd. 3790, London: DFEE.

—— (1999a) *Creativity, Culture and Education: Report of the National Advisory Committee on Creative and Cultural Education*, London: DFEE.

—— (1999b) *Financial Support for Students*, London: DFEE.

—— (1999c) *All Our Futures*, Report of the National Advisory Committee on Creative and Cultural Education, London: DFEE.

—— (2001) *Schools: Building on Success*, London: DFEE.

Department for Education and Employment and the Qualifications and Curriculum Authority (1999) *Citizenship: Key Stages 3–4 (The National Curriculum for England)*, London: DFEE and QCA.

Dudley, J. (1999) 'Higher Education Policy and the Learning Citizen', in A. Petersen, I. Barns, J. Dudley and P. Harris (eds) *Poststructuralism, Citizenship and Social Policy*, London: Routledge.

Esland, G., Esland, K., Murphy, M. and Yarrow, K. (1999) 'Managerializing Organizational Culture', in J. Ahier and G. Esland (eds) *Education, Training and the Future of Work*, vol. 1, London: Routledge.

Evans, G. R. and Gill, J. (2001) *Universities and Students*, London: Kogan Page.

Faulks, K. (1998) *Citizenship in Modern Britain*, Edinburgh: Edinburgh University Press.

Flew, A. (2000) *Education for Citizenship*, London: The Institute of Economic Affairs.

Foot, P. (1984) *Red Shelley*, London: Bookmarks.

Forsyth, A. and Furlong, A. (2000) *Socioeconomic Disadvantage and Access to Higher Education*, Bristol: Policy Press.

Frank, R. H. and Cook, P. J. (1996) *The Winner Takes All Society*, New York: The Free Press.

Frazer, E. (2000) 'Citizenship Education: Anti-political Culture and Political Education in Great Britain', *Political Studies*, 48: 88–103.

Freedland, M. (2001) 'The Marketization of Public Services', in C. Crouch, K. Eder and D. Tambini (eds) *Citizenship, Markets and the State*, Oxford: Oxford University Press.

Gamarnikow, E. and Green, A. (2000) 'Citizenship, Education and Social Capital', in D. Lawton, J. Cairns and R. Gardner (eds) *Education for Citizenship*, London: Continuum.

Giddens, A. (1982) *Profiles and Critiques in Social Theory*, London: Macmillan.

—— (1998) *The Third Way: The Renewal of Social Democracy*, Cambridge: Polity Press.

—— (2000a) *The Third Way and its Critics*, Cambridge: Polity Press.

—— (2000b) 'Citizenship in the Global Era', in N. Pearce and J. Hallgarten (eds) *Tomorrow's Citizens: Critical Debates in Citizenship and Education*, London: Institute of Public Policy Research.

Giese, R. (1999) 'School Board's Equity Policy Divides Even More', *Toronto Star*, 2 January: 2.

Goldthorpe, J. H. (1996) 'Class Analysis and the Reorientation of Class Theory: The Case of Persisting Differentials in Educational Attainment', *British Journal of Sociology*, 45: 481–505.

Goldthorpe, J. H., Lockwood, D., Bechhofer, F. and Platt, J. (1968a) *The Affluent Worker: Industrial Attitudes and Behaviour*, Cambridge: Cambridge University Press.

—— (1968b) *The Affluent Worker: Political Attitudes and Behaviour*, Cambridge: Cambridge University Press.

—— (1969) *The Affluent Worker in the Class Structure*, Cambridge: Cambridge University Press.

Habermas, J. (1989) *The Structural Transformation of the Public Sphere*, Cambridge: Polity Press.

Halsey, A. H. (1978) *Change in British Society*, Oxford: Oxford University Press.

—— (1992) *The Decline of Donnish Dominion: The British Academic Professions in the Twentieth Century*, Oxford: Clarendon Press.

Hansard (1989) *Parliamentary Debates*, vol. 158, columns 388–9, London: The Stationery Office.

Harrison, T. (1976) *Living Through the Blitz*, London: Collins.

Heater, D. (1990) *Citizenship: The Civic Ideal in World History, Politics and Education*, London: Longman.

Hebdige, R. (1990) 'Fax to the Future', *Marxism Today*, January: 18–23.

Henkel, M. (1997) 'Academic Values and the University as Corporate Enterprise', *Higher Education Quarterly*, 5, 2: 134–43.

Hennessy, P. (1993) *Never Again: Britain 1945–1951*, London: Vintage Books.

Hindess, B. (1987) *Freedom, Equality and the Market: Arguments on Social Policy*, London: Tavistock Publications.

Hirschmann, A. O. (1970) *Exit, Voice and Loyalty, Responses to Decline in Firms, Organisations and States*, Cambridge, MA: Harvard University Press.

Hirst, P. and Thompson, G. (1996) *Globalization in Question*, Cambridge: Polity Press.

—— (2000) 'Globalization in One Country? The Peculiarities of the British', *Economy and Society*, 29, 3: 335–56.

Hogan, D. (1997) 'The Logic of Protection: Citizenship, Justice and Political Community', in K. Kennedy (ed.) *Citizenship Education and the Modern State*, London: Falmer Press.

Howarth, A. (1991) 'Market Forces in Higher Education', *Higher Education Quarterly*, 45: 5–13.

Hurd, D. (1988) 'Citizenship in the Tory Democracy', *The New Statesman*, 29 April: 14.

—— (1989) 'Freedom Will Flourish where Citizens Accept Responsibility', *The Independent*, 13 September: 7.

Hutton, W. (1995) *The State We're In*, London: Jonathan Cape.

—— (1997) *The State to Come*, London: Vintage Books.

Ignatieff, M. (1994) *Blood and Belonging: Journey into the New Nationalism*, London: Vintage Books.

Institute for Employment Studies (2001) *The Annual Graduate Review, Report 374*, London: IES.

Isin, E. F. and Wood, P. (1999) *Citizenship and Identity*, London: Sage.

Israel, J. (2001) *Radical Enlightenment*, Oxford: Oxford University Press.

Jackson, B. and Marsden, D. (1966) *Education and the Working Class*, revised edition, Harmondsworth: Penguin Books.

Jameson, F. (1984) 'Postmodernism, or the Cultural Logic of Late Capitalism', *New Left Review*, 146: 53–92.

Jordan, B. (1998) *The New Politics of Welfare*, London: Sage.

Keane, J. (1995) *Tom Paine: A Political Life*, London: Bloomsbury.

Kelly, J. (2001) 'Demand Rises for Places in US Colleges', *Financial Times*, 18 May: 13.

Kymlicka, W. (1995) *Multicultural Citizenship*, Oxford: Clarendon Press.

Kymlicka, W. and Norman, W. (eds) (2000) *Citizenship in Diverse Societies*, Oxford: Oxford University Press.

Lasch, C. (1995) *The Revolt of the Elites and the Betrayal of Democracy*, New York: W. W. Norton and Company.

Levacic, R. (1995) *Local Management of Schools: Analysis and Practice*, Buckingham: Open University Press.

Lewicka, K. and McLaughlin, T. H. (2001) 'Education for European Identity and European Citizenship', in J. Ibanez-Martin and G. Jover (eds) *European Educational Politics: In Search of a Pedagogical Project from Maastricht to Amsterdam*, Dordrecht: Kluwer.

Lipset, S. M. and Marks, G. (2000) *It Didn't Happen Here: Why Socialism Failed in the United States*, New York: Norton.

McLaughlin, T. H. (1997) 'Education for Democracy and the Formation of National Identity', in D. Bridges (ed.) *Education, Democracy and Democratic Citizenship: Philosophy in a Changing World*, London: Routledge.

Macpherson, C. (1964) *The Political Theory of Possessive Individualism*, Oxford: Oxford University Press.

Macpherson, W. *et al.* (1999) *The Stephen Lawrence Enquiry*, London: The Stationery Office.

Margison, S. (1997) 'Investment in the Self: The Government of Student Financing in Australia', *Studies in Higher Education*, 22, 2: 119–31.

Marshall, T. H. (1950) *Citizenship and Social Class*, Cambridge: Cambridge University Press.

Marshall, T. H. and Bottomore, T. (1992) *Citizenship and Social Class*, London: Pluto Press.

Metcalf, H. (1997) *Class and Higher Education: The Participation of Young People from Lower Social Classes*, London: Council for Industry and Higher Education.

Middleton, C. (2000) 'Models of State and Market in the "Modernisation" of Higher Education', *British Journal of Sociology of Education*, 21, 4: 537–54.

Miller, D. (1995a) *On Nationalism*, Oxford: Clarendon Press.

—— (1995b) *Acknowledging Consumption: A Review of New Studies*, London: Routledge.

—— (2000a) 'Citizenship: What Does it Mean and Why is it Important?' in N. Pearce and J. Hallgarten (eds) *Tomorrow's Citizens: Critical Debates in Citizenship Education*, London: Institute for Public Policy Research.

—— (2000b) *Citizenship and National Identity*, Cambridge: Polity Press.

Moore, R. (1996) 'Back to the Future: The Problem of Change and the Possibilities of Advance in the Sociology of Education', *British Journal of Sociology of Education*, 17, 2: 145–61.

Moore, R. and Muller, J. (1999) 'The Discourse of "Voice" and the Problem of Knowledge in the Sociology of Education', *British Journal of Sociology of Education*, 20, 2: 189–206.

Mulgan, G. (1994) Lecture for the Institute for Citizenship Studies, London School of Economics, 8 September.

Nairn, T. (1988) *The Enchanted Glass: Britain and its Monarchy*, London: Radius.

National Committee of Enquiry into Higher Education (1997) *First Report*, London: Department for Education and Employment.

National Union of Students (1992) *NUS Student's Charter*, London: NUS.

Newman, J. and Clarke, J. (1994) 'Going Out of Business? The Managerialization of Public Services', in J. Clarke, A. Cochrane and E. McLaughlin (eds) *Managing Social Policy*, London: Sage.

Norbrook, D. (1999) *Writing the English Republic*, Cambridge: Cambridge University Press.

O'Hear, A. (1999) 'Enter the New Robot Citizens', *The Daily Mail*, 14 May: 12.

Ohmae, K. (1995) *The End of the Nation State: The Rise of Regional Economies*, London: HarperCollins.

Opacic, S. (1994) 'The Student Learning Experience in the Mid-1990's', in S. Haselgrove (ed.) *The Student Experience*, Buckingham: The Society for Research into Higher Education and the Open University Press.

Organisation for Economic Co-operation and Development (1996) *Internationalisation of Higher Education*, Paris: OECD.

Osler, A. and Starkey, H. (2000) 'Citizenship, Human Rights and Cultural Diversity', in A. Osler (ed.) *Citizenship and Democracy in Schools: Diversity, Identity, Equality*, Stoke on Trent: Trentham Books.

Paterson, L. (2000) 'Civil Society and Democratic Renewal', in S. Baron, J. Field and T. Schuller (eds) *Social Capital: Critical Perspectives*, Oxford: Oxford University Press.

Petrovic, J. (1999) 'Moral Democratic Education and Homosexuality: Censoring Morality', *Journal of Moral Education*, 28: 201–9.

Pimlott, B. (1992) 'Fifty Years on from Beveridge', *The Independent*, 1 December: 12.

Pirie, M. and Worcester, R. (2000) *The Big Turn-off*, London: Adam Smith Institute.

Plant, R. (1990) 'Citizenship and Rights', in R. Plant and N. Barry (eds) *Citizenship and Rights: Two Views*, London: Institute of Economic Affairs.

Porter, R. (2000) *Enlightenment: Britain and the Creation of the Modern World*, London: Allen Lane.

Poster, M. (1990) *The Mode of Information: Post-structuralism and Social Context*, Cambridge: Polity Press.

Pugsley, L. (1998) 'Throwing your Brains at it: Higher Education, Markets and Choice', *International Studies in Sociology of Education*, 8, 1: 71–90.

Qualifications and Curriculum Authority (2000) *Citizenship at Key Stages 3 and 4: Initial Guidance for Schools*, London: Qualifications and Curriculum Authority.

—— (2001) *Citizenship: A Scheme of Work for Key Stage 3*, London: Qualifications and Curriculum Authority.

Ranson, S. (1996) 'Markets or Democracy for Education', in J. Ahier, B. Cosin and M. Hales (eds) *Diversity and Change*, London: Routledge.

Rawls, J. (1993) *Political Liberalism*, New York: Columbia University Press.

—— (1999) 'The Idea of Public Reason Revisited', in J. Rawls, *The Law of Peoples*, Cambridge, MA: Harvard University Press.

Reay, D. (1998) ' "Always Knowing" and "Ever Being Sure": Familial and Institutional Habituses and Higher Education Choice', *Journal of Education Policy*, 13, 4: 519–29.

Reich, R. (1991) *The Work of Nations: A Blueprint for the Future*, London: Simon and Schuster.

—— (1998) 'Why the Rich Are Getting Richer and the Poor Poorer', in A. H. Halsey, H. Lauder, P. Brown and A. S. Wells (eds) *Education, Culture, Economy and Society*, Oxford: Oxford University Press, reprinted from Reich, R. B. (1991) *The Work of Nations: A Blueprint for the Future*, London: Simon and Schuster.

Robertson, D. (2000) 'Students as Consumers', in P. Scott (ed.) *Higher Education Reformed*, London: The Falmer Press.

Rose, N. (1993) 'Government, Authority and Expertise in Advanced Liberalism', *Economy and Society*, 22, 3: 283–99.

—— (1999a) *Powers of Freedom: Reframing Political Thought*, Cambridge: Cambridge University Press.

—— (1999b) 'Inventiveness in Politics': Review of A. Giddens (1998) *The Third Way: The Renewal of Social Democracy*, Cambridge: Polity Press, *Economy and Society*, 28, 3: 467–93.

Runnymede Trust (2000) *The Future of Multi-Ethnic Britain: Report of the Commission on the Future of Multi-Ethnic Britain* (The Parekh Report), London: Profile Books.

Rustin, M. (1994) 'Flexibility in Higher Education', in R. Burrows and B. Loader (eds) *Towards a Post-Fordist Welfare State?*, London: Routledge.

Savage, M., Barlow, J., Dickens, P. and Fielding, T. (1992) *Property, Bureaucracy, and Culture*, London: Routledge.

SCAD (1997) *The Amsterdam Treaty: A Comprehensive Guide: The Union and the Citizen* (http://euro2.eu.int/scadplus/leg/en/lvb/a12000.htm).

Scott, A. (1997) 'Introduction – Globalization: Social Process or Political Rhetoric?', in A. Scott (ed.) *The Limits of Globalization*, London: Routledge.

Scott, P. (1998) 'Massification, Internationalization and Globalization', in P. Scott (ed.) *The Globalization of Higher Education*, Buckingham: Open University Press.

Scruton, R. (1998) 'Where Marx was Right and Thatcher Wrong, *The Independent on Sunday*, 16 August: 24.

Selbourne, D. (1994) *Principle of Duty: An Essay on the Foundation of Civic Order*, London: Sinclair-Stevenson.

Shapin, S. (1994) *A Social History of Truth*, Chicago: University of Chicago Press.

Shumar, W. (1979) *College for Sale*, London: Falmer.

Silver, H. and Silver, P. (1997) *Students: Changing Roles, Changing Lives*, Buckingham: Society for Research into Higher Education and Open University Press.

Slater, D. R. (1997) *Consumer Culture and Modernity*, Cambridge: Polity Press.

Slaughter, S. (1998) 'National Higher Education Policies in a Global Economy', in J. Currie and J. Newson (eds) *Universities and Globalization*, Thousand Oaks, CA: Sage Publications.

St. Clair, W. (1990) *The Godwins and the Shelleys*, London: Faber & Faber.

Straw, J. (1998) 'Building Social Cohesion, Order and Inclusion in a Market Economy', speech to the Nexus Conference on 'Mapping Out the Third Way', 3 July, London.

Taylor, C. (1992) 'The Politics of Recognition', in C. Taylor, *The Politics of Recognition (with commentary by A. Gutman, S. C. Rockerfeller, M. Walzer and S. Wolf)*, Princeton, NJ: Princeton University Press.

Taylor, M. (2001) 'Next Stop Utopia ... but it'll Cost us', *The Observer*, 19 August: 24.

Thatcher, M. (1989) *The Revival of Britain*, London: HarperCollins.

—— (1992) 'Don't Undo My Work', *Newsweek*, 27 April: 37.

Thompson, E. P. (1965) 'The Peculiarities of the English', in R. Miliband and J. Saville (eds) *The Socialist Register 1965*, London: The Merlin Press.

Thompson, J. (1994) 'The Theory of the Public Sphere: A Critical Appraisal', in J. Thompson (ed) *The Polity Reader in Cultural Theory*, Cambridge: Polity Press.

Titmuss, R. M. (1950) *Problems of Social Policy*, London: HMSO and Longmans Green.

Tooley, J. (1997) 'Higher Education Without the State', in A. Seville and J. Tooley (eds) *The Debate on Higher Education*, London: Institute of Economic Affairs.

—— (2000) *Reclaiming Education*, London: Cassell.

Townsend, P. (1996) *A Poor Future: Can we Counter Growing Poverty in Britain and across the World?*, London: Lemos and Crane.

Townsend, P. and Gordon, D. (2000) 'Introduction: The Measurement of Poverty in Europe', in D. Gordon and P. Townsend (eds) *Breadline Europe: The Measurement of Poverty*, Bristol: The Policy Press.

Tritter, J. (1994) 'The Citizen's Charter: Opportunities for Users' Perspectives?', *The Political Quarterly*, 65: 397–414.

Turner, B. S. (1989) 'From Postindustrial Society to Modern Politics: The Political Sociology of Daniel Bell', in J. Gibbins (ed.) *Contemporary Political Culture: Politics in a Postmodern Age*, London: Sage.

—— (1990) 'Outline of a Theory of Citizenship', *Sociology*, 24, 2: 189–217.

—— (1993) 'Contemporary Problems in the Theory of Citizenship', in B. Turner (ed.) *Citizenship and Social Theory*, London: Sage.

UNITE (2002) *Student Living Report*, London: UNITE Group plc.

Van Gunsteren, H. (1978) 'Notes Towards a Theory of Citizenship', in F. Dallmyr (ed.) *From Contract to Community*, New York: Marcel Decker.

Walters, P. and Baldwin, E. (1998) 'Complicated Money: Funding Student Participation in Mass Higher Education', in D. Jary and M. Parker (eds) *The New Higher Education*, Stoke on Trent: Staffordshire University Press.

Wilkins, C. (1999) 'Making Good Citizens: The Social and Political Attitudes of PGCE Students', *Oxford Review of Education*, 25: 217–30.

Williams, J. (ed.) (1997) *Negotiating Access to Higher Education*, Buckingham: Society for Research into Higher Education and Open University Press.

Winn, S. and Stevenson, R. (1997) 'Student Loans: Are the Policy Objectives Being Achieved?', *Higher Education Quarterly*, 51, 2: 144–63.

Winter, R. (1999) 'The University of Life plc', in J. Ahier and G. Esland (eds) *Education, Training and the Future of Work*, vol. 1, London: Routledge.

Wooley, B. (1999) *The Bride of Science*, Basingstoke: Macmillan.

Worsthorne, P. (1959) 'Class and Conflict in British Foreign Policy', *Foreign Affairs*, xxxvii: 419–31.

Young, I. M. (1990) *Justice and the Politics of Difference*, Princeton, NJ: Princeton University Press.

Zine, J. (2001) ' "Negotiating Equity": The Dynamics of Minority Community Engagement in Constructing Inclusive Educational Policy', *Cambridge Journal of Education*, 31, 2: 239–69.

Index